El Stamp
København 1966

BRANWEN UERCH LYR

INSTITIÚID ÁRD-LÉINN
BHAILE ÁTHA CLIATH

MEDIEVAL AND MODERN WELSH SERIES

Published

I. PWYLL PENDEUIC DYUET
Edited by R. L. THOMSON. *Price 8s. 6d.*

II. BRANWEN UERCH LYR
Edited by DERICK S. THOMSON. *Price 8s. 6d.*

In preparation

KULHWCH AC OLWEN
Edited by IDRIS LL. FOSTER

MATH FAB MATHONWY
Edited by B. REES

MANAWYDAN FAB LLYR
Edited by A. O. H. JARMAN

DAFYDD AP GWILYM (selection)
Edited by THOMAS PARRY

POEMS OF THE CYNFEIRDD
Edited by J. E. CAERWYN WILLIAMS

HANES GRUFFYDD AP CYNAN
Edited by G. MELVILLE RICHARDS

OWEIN
Edited by R. L. THOMSON

LIFE OF S. DAVID
Edited by SIMON EVANS

POEMS OF THE CYWYDDWYR
Edited by E. I. ROWLANDS

YSTORI ALEXANDER A LODWIG
Edited by THOMAS JONES

MEDIAEVAL AND MODERN WELSH SERIES
Volume II

BRANWEN UERCH LYR

The Second of the Four Branches of the Mabinogi
edited from the White Book of Rhydderch
with variants from the Red Book of Hergest
and from Peniarth 6

by

DERICK S. THOMSON
Reader in Celtic
University of Aberdeen

THE DUBLIN INSTITUTE FOR
ADVANCED STUDIES
1961

PRINTED IN GREAT BRITAIN

PREFACE

THE main purpose of this book is to provide an edition of the story of Branwen which can be closely studied by those whose knowledge of Modern Welsh is not sufficient to give them free access to all the scholarly work that has been done on the text. The needs of such students have been specially kept in mind in the notes and the vocabulary as well as in the Introduction. But I have sought also to make the book serviceable for Welsh-speaking students by referring to material which has been published since Sir Ifor Williams's standard Welsh edition in *Pedeir Keinc y Mabinogi*.

The most considerable single contribution, since then, to a fuller understanding of the tale, is Mr. Proinsias Mac Cana's *Branwen Daughter of Llŷr*, which was published after I had written this book. Fortunately, there was time to refer to his discussion of many points. I have let my own introduction stand for the most part, but have added references to Mr. Mac Cana's book and some new paragraphs in which my indebtedness is always indicated. But these additions will not absolve any student of this text from reading *Branwen Daughter of Llŷr* for himself.

Sir Ifor Williams has placed all the younger generation of Welsh scholars deeply in his debt (as indeed he has placed an older generation also), and I must acknowledge my own indebtedness. Others will share with me the recollection of a time when his notes to texts presented almost as much difficulty as the texts themselves. It is to be hoped that non-Welsh students will continue to undergo the wholesome discipline of learning Modern Welsh if only to gain an understanding of what these notes contain. The notes in this book are offered as *scalae primae*.

PREFACE

I wish to express my indebtedness to Professor Idris Foster and Professor Myles Dillon. Professor Foster read my typescript, and made detailed suggestions, many of which have been incorporated in the book; Professor Dillon, besides making suggestions, may be said to have nursed it into such health as it has after a sickly and uncertain beginning some five years ago.

My grateful thanks are also due to Professor J. E. Caerwyn Williams, of Bangor, with whom I have corresponded over certain points, and to Mr. Robert L. Thomson, of Leeds, for reading the proofs.

DERICK S. THOMSON

King's College
Old Aberdeen
December 1958

CONTENTS

INTRODUCTION   ix
> Editions of Text and Translations, ix; Manuscript Sources of the Text of *Branwen*, ix; Orthography, xi; Grammatical and Syntactical, xiii; Summary of the Scheme of the Four Branches, and the relationship of *Branwen* to that scheme, xxi; External Influences on *Branwen*, xxxiii; Literary Quality and Style of *Branwen*, xlii; Composition of the Text, xlvi.

BIBLIOGRAPHY   xlix

ABBREVIATIONS (Grammatical, &c.)   lii

BRANWEN UERCH LYR   1

NOTES   19

APPENDIX (Extract from Peniarth 6)   42

VOCABULARY   44

INDEX OF PERSONAL NAMES   77

INDEX OF PLACE-NAMES   78

INTRODUCTION

Editions of Text and Translations

THE text of *Branwen* has been published in its two main versions in the diplomatic transcripts of Sir John Rhŷs and J. Gwenogvryn Evans, *The Text of the Mabinogion and other Welsh Tales from the Red Book of Hergest* (Oxford, 1887) and of J. Gwenogvryn Evans, *The White Book Mabinogion* (Pwllheli, 1907). A German edition of the Four Branches of the Mabinogi, *Die vier Zweige des Mabinogi*, was published by L. Mühlhausen (Halle, 1925). The standard Welsh edition, based on the text of the White Book, was published by Sir Ifor Williams in his *Pedeir Keinc y Mabinogi* (Cardiff, 1930); this edition includes a transcript of a short extract from the story, as found in Peniarth MS. 6. This is given also in Evans, WBM 279–80. Various translations and renderings have been published, including the following: Lady Charlotte Guest, *The Mabinogion from the Llyfr Coch o Hergest, and other ancient Welsh manuscripts, with an English Translation and Notes* (London, 1838–49); a French translation by J. Loth, *Les Mabinogion* (2nd ed., Paris, 1913); T. P. Ellis and J. Lloyd, *The Mabinogion* (Oxford, 1929); a modern Welsh rendering by T. H. Parry-Williams, *Pedair Cainc y Mabinogi wedi eu diweddaru* (Cardiff, 1937); Gwyn Jones and Thomas Jones, *The Mabinogion, A New Translation, &c.* (London, 1948).

Manuscript Sources of the Text of Branwen

The text of the Four Branches of the Mabinogi is contained in two closely related manuscripts, the earlier being the White Book of Rhydderch (Peniarth MSS. 4 and 5), the later the Red Book of Hergest (Jesus Coll. MS. CXI). The White Book recension of the Four Branches was dated by Dr. Gwenogvryn

Evans, on palaeographical evidence, *c.* 1300–25, and the Red Book recension *c.* 1375–1425. Two short extracts from these stories occur in an earlier manuscript, Peniarth 6, which Dr. Evans dated *c.* 1235. One of these fragments is from the story of *Branwen*, and it is reproduced in an appendix to this edition.[1] The manuscripts Peniarth 6 and the White Book of Rhydderch are in the National Library of Wales, and the Red Book of Hergest is in the Bodleian Library in Oxford.

There is no general agreement on the relationship of these three manuscripts. It is clear that the relationship is so close that they cannot be regarded as different recensions. It is almost as clear that none of these manuscripts is a copy of another of the three. The closer relationship of W and R becomes evident from a comparison with the two passages in P. Apart from small orthographical variations there are approximately a hundred readings in the passages from P where W differs from P.[2] In these cases R usually agrees with the text of W as regards word order, but differs slightly in spelling, and sometimes gives a later form instead of an old one, or alters a strange word for a more common one. R never agrees with P against W except fortuitously in a point of orthography or mutation, apart from the form *dyro* common to R and P and given as *doro* in W. Lacunae in W are generally reproduced in R. The most likely conclusion is that P and W had a common original. There may, however, have been an intermediate copy between this original and W, and R may have used this copy also, emending it and altering the orthography in a manner different from that of the scribe of W. Variations in orthography are more fully discussed below.

The date of the original recension, from which P, W, and R ultimately derive, can be pushed back well beyond 1235, the approximate date of P. For a variety of reasons, which have

[1] pp. 42–43.
[2] Ifor Williams discusses these points fully in PKM viii–xii.

been summarized by Mr. R. L. Thomson,[1] it seems likely that the Four Branches assumed roughly their present form in the second half of the eleventh century.[2] The possibility should be borne in mind, however, that certain additions may have been made in the intermediate version from which W and R derive, e.g. in such episodes as the description of the Iron House, which may be an addition dating from the twelfth century.[3]

Orthography

The orthography of the two main manuscript sources varies widely. In the following list the most frequently recurring variations are noted. The White Book form is given first with an indication, within brackets, of the value of the letters in a similar context in Mod. W.; the Red Book form is then given, and a tally of the number of occurrences in our text is added.

W *u* (*u, w, f, b* (len.), *m* (len.)), R *v* (88); W *n* (*n, nn*), R *nn* (44), and W *nn* (*n, nn*), R *n* (6)—the variation here is not very significant, although on the whole the usage of R is closer to that of Mod. W.; W *y* (*y, e*), R *e* (40), and W *e*, R *y* (26)—neither manuscript approaches consistency within itself, and the most satisfactory explanation is probably that W and R both used the same exemplar, which used widely the old spelling of *e* for *y* (W, however, retains *e* for the definite article more frequently than R does); W *d* medial or final (*d*), R *t* (38), and W *t* (*t*?), R *d* (2); W *t* initial (usually len. *t*), R *d* (12); W *t* (*t*), R *tt* (20); W *th* (*dd*), R *t* (10), and W *t*, R *th* (1); W *gu* (*gw*), R *gw* (23); W *nh* (*nn*), R *nn* (26); W *f* (*ff*), R *ff* (14); W *u* medial (*f*),

[1] *Pwyll* xii–xvi.

[2] W. J. Gruffydd seems to have been inclined to attribute the authorship of the Four Branches to Bleddri, a Welsh *cyfarwydd* of the first half of the eleventh century (RC xxxiii, 180–3). But in *Rhiannon* he was more guarded, and less specific. For a different suggestion, see p. xxxi, n. 1.

[3] p. xxxvi below. Mac Cana, in *Branwen Daughter of Llŷr*, would seem to prefer a date not much anterior to A.D. 1100. See, for example, the note on l. 75 of the text.

R *f* (10); W *y* (*i*), R *i* (16), and W *i* (*i*), R *y* (12); W *f* (*ph*), R *ph* (6); W *-ngh-*, R *-ng-* (6); W *-ngh-*, R *-gh-* (7); W *-ng-*, R *-g-* (4); W *-gh-*, R *-ng-* (1); W *s* (*s, ss*), R *ss* (6); W *l*, R *ll* (5).); W has *meirych* as against R's *meirch* (9);[1] W *wy*, R *hwy* (4); W *-aeth*, R *-yaeth* (4); W *-yssant* (termination of past 3 pl.), R *-assant* (12), R *-yassant* (5). There is considerable variation in the writing of initial mutations: in addition to examples given above, we may note W *b*, R *p* (12), and W *p*, R *b* (5); W *uygw-*, R *vyg gw-* (4); W *k*, R *g* (2), &c. The general pattern is somewhat confused; there is a tendency for the forms of R to resemble more closely those of Mod. W. than do those of W, but it is doubtful if the orthographical evidence gives support to the theory that W occupies an intermediate position between R and W's exemplar. The close relationship of W and R cannot, however, be doubted, and probably we should conclude that both are edited versions rather than slavish copies of the same exemplar. If this is so, we must conclude further that R is the more careless copy, and that the scribe of R probably understood his original less well than the scribe of W did. Examples of inexact copying can be seen at ll. 184–5 (where the scribe jumps from the first occurrence of *megineu* to the second, omitting the whole passage *a oed wedy eu gossot ygylch y ty a gwr a pob dwy uegin a dechreu chwythu y megineu*), ll. 258–60 and 271–2. For what look like attempts at editing obscure passages, see the notes on ll. 113, 124, 131, and 261–2.

The two short extracts from Peniarth 6 (one of these from the story of *Branwen*) throw interesting light on the relationship of the manuscripts. On the whole the orthography of R is closer to P than that of W. Thus, as in R, the use of *e* is common in P where W has *y*, but W and R generally agree in writing *yn*, *yna* as against P's *en*, *ena*. W's *u* frequently corresponds to P's *f*, and R has a number of instances of *f* in this context, although usually preferring *v*; P has *gygor* as against

[1] See note, l. 66.

INTRODUCTION   xiii

W's *gynghor* (cf. R's *g* as against W's *ng*); P has *nn* as against W's *nh*, *ff* as against W's *f*, *gw*- as against W's *gu*-, *ph* as against W's *f*, and *-t* as against W's *-d*, although the usage of P is not consistent in this case. We have noted above R's preference for such endings as *-assam*, *-assant* in the 1 and 3 pl. of the past tense, where W prefers *-yssam*, *-yssant*. There is only one instance of such a verbal form in the P extract from *Branwen*, and one in the extract from *Manawydan*, and both use the ending *-assant*. P and R agree in writing *bont* rather than *pont* (294). With regard to other than orthographical variants the evidence is not clear. Thus W and R agree in writing *racdu* (312), as against P's *racdunt*, *parth* as against P's *stlys* (319), and *yn y* as against P's *or* (319). W and P agree in writing *ehegyr* as against R's *ebrwyd* (311). P and R agree in writing *dyro* as against W's *doro* (320) and *ureithell/vreithell* as against W's *ureichell* (337).

If we call the eleventh-century original A, and the manuscript which links W and R to it B, we may conjecture that P derives independently from A, that W is a copy of B with modernization of orthography, and that R is a more careless and less critical copy which nevertheless retains a number of the orthographical features of B (as P does those of A), but in other respects modernizes even more than W does. But it should be remembered that this conjecture is made in the light of evidence which, as regards P, is admittedly scanty.

Grammatical and Syntactical

Without aiming at completeness of treatment, examples of certain grammatical and syntactical usages in our text are collected here. This review may be supplemented by a study of the standard textbooks referred to in the Bibliography.

Nouns. Case inflexions of the noun were lost at a very early period (about the first half of the sixth century A.D., according to K. H. Jackson) and broadly speaking, the only surviving inflexions are those indicating number. The plurals of certain nouns in our text differ from the Mod. W. forms, e.g. *broder* is used as the plural, and also as the dual, of *brawt*; in Mod. W. this is affected to *brodyr*. Initial mutation survives from earlier feminine nominal and adjectival terminations, in such instances as *un uam* (5) and *uerch Ueli* as contrasted with *uab Mynogan* (8), where there is lenition after *merch* (f.) but not after *mab* (m.). A noun is usually lenited (i) in genitive relationship after a fem. noun, *Branwen uerch Lyr* (54–5), (ii) in apposition to a proper noun, *Bendigeiduran uab Llyr* (1), *Penardun uerch Ueli* (8), (iii) in apposition to another common noun, *y Wern uab Matholwch, dy nei ditheu, uab dy chwaer* (302–3).

Adjectives. Adjectives are for the most part compared regularly, e.g. comparative, *tebygach* (124), *digriuach, hyurydach* (443), and superlative, *teccaf* (46). There are a small number of adjectives which have irregular comparison, as *mawr*, compar. *mwy* (72), superl. *mwyaf* (11); *da*, compar. *gwell*, superl. *goreu*. More variety exists in the case of equative adjectives: the equative degree may be expressed by means of the termination *-et:* as *uychanet* (134) (eq. of *bychan*), or by *-et* together with preceding *kyn* (*gyn*), as *gyn anwylet* (83), *gynebrwydet ac* (352). Strictly speaking, the adj. is eq. only when *kyn* precedes it. There are several instances of equative adjj. or the equivalent of equative adjj. being formed by prefixing *ky-*, *cy-* (also *kyf-*, *kym-*) to nouns, e.g. *cyhyt* (114), *gyniuer* (454), *kyuurd* (83). Certain adjectives have an irregular equative form, based on a different root, as *kystal* (71), *kymeint* (155). Three ways of expressing the equative notion are exemplified in (83), *morwyn gystal, kyuurd, gyn anwylet gan y chenedyl*.

Infixed pronouns. The infixed personal pronouns, used objectively, occur fairly frequently, generally in the 3 sg. Examples of *'e* and *'y* are *mi a'e managaf y ti* (155), *a phawb o'r a'e guelei* (356); the infixed pronoun is 3 pl. in *ac na wydat pwy a'e lladei* (419). Examples of the dependent genitive infixed pronoun after a conjunction are *ac yna kymryt y llythyr a'y edrych* (235) and *dyuot deu Wydel - - - - a'y uwrw* (383). Examples of inf. *'s*, again 3 sg., are *pei ys gwypwn* (92), *ac nys gadwn* (108), and *onys gwyr Branwen* (269).

The verb. Relics of the *s*-preterite are frequent, examples being the 3 sg. preterites *edewis* (340), *gelwis* (357), *welas* (366), *gynsynwys* (367), *peris* (391). The old *t*-preterite is more thinly represented, mainly by forms of *mynet* and *kymryt*, e.g. *aeth* (88) and *gymerth* (142); but also *(g)want* (365).

ry is used as a perfective particle (cf. Ir. *ro*) in *coet rywelsam ar y weilgi* (263), *a reuedawt rygyueryw a mi* (94).

Where the subject of a clause is a noun, a singular verb is normally used with a plural subject, as in Gaelic; an example in the text is *y nessawys y gwyr attunt* (25–26), but many examples occur in Med. W. of concord between verb and plural subject, e.g. *y kychwynassant yr yniueroed* (48). The form of the sentence *e kennadeu a aethant* (120), in which there is also concord between verb and subject, is different from that of the last instance: this is an example of what is called the 'abnormal' sentence, in which the subject or object of the verb, or an adverb or adverbial phrase, is placed at the beginning. In such an 'abnormal' sentence a singular verb may also be used with a plural subject, as in *A chenadeu a aeth* (88). Such usages should also be distinguished from that in *Sef kennadeu a aeth* (89), where *a* is the relative pronoun, which is always followed by a singular verb. Where the subject is a pronoun, expressed or understood, there is always concord between subject and verb, e.g. *Beth a wnant wy yna?* (68). In the sentence *y gwyr a wiscawd amdanunt ac a nessayssant* (19), the first clause is an example of the 'abnormal' word order, and in the second we have concord between plural verb and plural pronominal subject (understood).

Indirect statements are generally introduced by the vn. *bot*, e.g. *a phan welsant uot yn well* (59), *e chwedl a doeth . . . bot*

Matholwch yn adaw (87), *ac erbyn auory y uot yn gystal ac* ... (140), *guae ui uy mot yn achaws* ... (380). In the passage *a menegwch idaw, ef a geif march iach* ... (111), where the sense is future and where *bot* would not be used, *ef a geif march iach* may perhaps be regarded as intermediate between direct and indirect statement.

The verbal noun is often used in co-ordinate positions following a finite verb, thus, *e gwyr hynny a ymchwelwys* ... *a menegi* (105–6). The sense expressed is usually that of the past tense, as in the following example, where the first clause contains a pluperfect, *ac ual y guascassei benneu y rei ereill, guascu* ... (343–4). If is also used independently of either the auxiliary *gwneuthur* ('make, do') or a finite verb, e.g. *mynnu ymgyuathrachu a thidy* (35–36), *yn y lle trannoeth kymryt kynghor* (44), *guan y dan y meirych, a thorri* ... (73)[1]. *Gwneuthur* itself is used in this way, e.g. *a gwneuthur oed* ... (47). Apart from the instances in which a verbal noun appears as the object of *gwneuthur*, e.g. *bwrw badeu allan a wnaethont* (26–27), *kyuodi a orugant* (62), *rodi y mab ar uaeth a wnaethpwyt* (211–12), there are many examples of the use of the verbal noun in co-ordinate clauses, where a finite form of *gwneuthur* has been used in the main clause, e.g. *bwrw badeu allan a wnaethont wynteu, a nessau parth a'r tir, a chyuarch guell y'r brenhin* (26–28), *dilit y gyuedach a wnaethant ac ymdidan* (58–59), *meithryn ederyn drydwen a wnaeth hitheu* ... *a dyscu ieith idi, a menegi* ... (227–8).

Two other methods of expressing a finite tense without using a finite verb may be noted. Clauses containing the interj. *llyma* 'behold' are generally followed by the verbal noun preceded by *yn* and serving as a present participle, e.g. *llyma gennadeu Matholwch yn dyuot attaw ef* (298–9), *llyma gyweithyd yn kyuaruot ac wynt* (411–12). Frequently, when the verbal

[1] For a similar Irish usage, see P. L. Henry, *Lochlann* I, 93 and ZCP xxviii, 29.

noun is used instead of a finite verb, the agent, if a noun, is governed by the prep. *o*, which follows immediately on the verbal noun, e.g. *galw o Uendigeiduran y mab attaw* (354–5), *a chael o Uendigeiduran* (368), *goresgyn o Gaswallawn uab Beli Ynys y Kedyrn* (414). Similarly, a prepositional pronoun based on *o* may be used, *edrych oheni hitheu ar Iwerdon* (405). These examples seem to express past tenses; the pluperfect is similarly expressed, with the addition of the prep. *gwedy*, e.g. *guedy gorwed ohonaw ef ar traws yr auon* (296). The prep. pron. based on *i* is used to denote the agent of the action expressed by the verbal noun in *emystynnu idaw ynteu yn y peir* (384).

These are the commonest ways of expressing the narrative tenses in the prose of our text. The use of the dramatic present is less common in the prose of the Mabinogi than in Mid. Ir. prose.

The substantive verb and the copula. As in the Gaelic dialects, the syntax of the substantive verb and of the copula is somewhat complex. Forms of the vb. *bot* can be used to perform the function of a copula, as *negessawl yw wrthyt ti* 'he is a messenger to you' (34), *a honno oed tryded prif rieni* (45–46), *mi a uydaf pont* 'I shall be a bridge' (294), or negatively, *nit wyt gystal ymdidanwr heno* 'you are not as good a conversationalist tonight' (135). With inversion of the word-order, and consequent emphasis of the opening words of the clause, we get *teccaf morwyn yn y byt oed* 'the fairest maiden in the world she was' (46). An example of an interrogative sentence in which *oed* is used as a copula is *beth oed y mynyd a welit* 'what was the mountain that was seen (people were seeing)?' (275). *yw* is used as a copula in these sentences: *Meirych Matholwch . . . yw y rei hyn* 'these are Matholwch's horses' (67–68), *beth yw hynny?* 'what is that?' (94–95), *mwy yw* 'it is greater' (102).

The copula *ys*, corresponding etymologically to Gael. *is*, is of somewhat rare occurrence in our text, but there is one example at ll. 362–3, *ys anhebic a gyflauan . . . a wnaf i* 'Unlikely is the (kind of) outrage . . . that I shall commit'. It is more common in composition with the conjunction *o* 'if', e.g. *os da genhyt ti* 'if you please, if you approve' (37) (cf. Gael. *mas math leat-sa*, which is a parallel construction), *os uy gwaradwydaw a uynhynt* 'if it is my insulting they desired' (82). The copula *ys* enters into composition with the pron. *ef*, giving the form *ys(s)ef*, and the one which appears in our text, *sef*. It is used at the beginning of its clause, sometimes, as in the first example below, to show unequivocally that the verbal noun is intended to be emphasized. It may be used nominally and adjectivally, or adverbially: (*a*) nominally and adjectivally, *sef a wnaeth Efnyssyen dyuot* 'this is what E. did, come', or 'what E. did was to come' (331); *sef kennadeu a aeth, Idic uab Anarawc ...* 'these are the messengers who went, Idic son of A ...' (89); (*b*) adverbially, *sef y clywei arueu am benn hwnnw* 'now he felt armour on that one's head' (344–5).

Besides being used as the independent form of the present tense of the substantive verb (as in *mae genhym ni chwedleu ryued* 'we have wonderful tidings' (262–3), *mae* is used in interrogative sentences in the sense of 'where is?', e.g. *mae dy gynghor am bont?* 'where is your counsel regarding a bridge?' (292–3).

oes, a dependent form of the present, is used in negative and interrogative sentences, generally with an indefinite subject, e.g. *nyt oes gynghor namyn kilyaw* 'there is no counsel save to flee' (284–5); *a oes gennwch chwi chwedleu?* 'have you (any) news?' and the answer to this is *nac oes* 'no' (412–13).

yssyd is the relative form of the present of the verb 'to be'; it is used in relative clauses, e.g. *a thorri y bont yssyd ar yr auon* 'and to break the bridge that is on the river' (286), *beth yssyd yn y boly hwnn?* lit. 'what is it that is in this bag?' (334). This form is to be distinguished from the non-relative form written *yssit* in our text, *yssit yn y boly hwnn amryw ulawt* 'there is in this bag diverse kinds of flour' (347), (see Pedersen ii, 426, 428; Morris-Jones, WG § 189).

Structure of the clause and the sentence. Unlike Mod. W., in

INTRODUCTION

which a norm of verb–subject–object can be discerned in the word-order of the clause or sentence, Med. W. prose allows itself considerable freedom of word-order, a freedom which is turned to advantage for stylistic purposes by the redactor of *Branwen*. The instances in which the verb occurs at the beginning of the clause, apart from those where the verb is in the imperative, are comparatively infrequent. Examples are l. 167, *y kymereis inheu wyntwy arnaf* (verb, subject, object), and l. 175, *E dodeis inheu ar gynghor uy gwlat* (verb, subject, complement). More common are:

(*a*) object first:

> *a chynghor a gymerwn ninheu* (39),
> *a'r gyuedach a dechreussant* (58),
> *cwbyl waradwyd a geueis* (93),
> *y ulwydyn honno a duc hi yn glotuawr* (207–8),
> *ac ystryw a wnaeth y Gwydyl* (328),

where, in the cases where the subject is expressed, the word-order is object, verb, subject.

(*b*) subject first:

> *yr atteb hwnnw a aeth* (40),
> *e chwedyl a doeth at Uatholwch* (78),
> *a reuedawt rygyueryw a mi* (94),
> *a chwi a uydwch ar y ford* (393–4),

where the word-order is subject, verb, complement.

(*c*) complement first:

> *ac y'r llys y deuthant* (125–6),
> *yn hela yd oedwn* (156).

The word-order of subject, verb, object/complement is, however, regular in sentences expressing a wish, e.g.

> *Duw a dalo yt* (137–8),
> *Duw a rodo da ywch* (261).

The preverbal particles *a*, *y*, and *yd* are widely used before the verb, as may be observed from the examples quoted above. *yd* is frequently used also before the forms of the imperfect of *bot*.

In negative sentences the verb generally comes immediately after the negative, e.g. *ny angassei Uendigeituran* (56–7), *ni duc neb kyrch waeth* (93). Similarly in conditional and concessive sentences, e.g. *eithyr na byd llyueryd ganthaw* (141), *ony wdosti* (154), *ony allaf i ue hun cael* ... (306–7). An apparently exceptional order is that of *onyt y neges a geif* (34–5), but here *onyt* contains the copula, and *a geif* is a co-ordinate clause.

In interrogative clauses the verb (preceded by the particle *a* or *yld*), follows immediately after the interrogative word or phrase, e.g. *beth* ... *a uynnhei ef?* (32–3), *pan doeth yti y peir* ...? (148), *pa delw* ... *yd erbynneisti wynteu?* (193–4). It is perhaps worth noting that the answer to a question, as this last, sometimes does not contain a finite verb in the principal clause, e.g. *eu rannu ym pob lle yn y kyuoeth* (194).

Relative and paratactic constructions. The lack of a fully developed system of relative pronouns, with oblique cases, results at times in a loose articulation of the sentence, which can be easily paralleled in Irish and Scottish Gaelic. The relative clause may be separated from its antecedent, as in the following example, *ac nachaf yn ardiawc gan Uendigeituran y(r) ymdidan, ac yn drist, a gaei gan Uatholwch, a'y lywenyt yn wastat kyn no hynny* (131–3), where *a gaei gan Uatholwch* is separated from its antecedent *y(r) ymdidan*. Examples of paratactic constructions are *Ny doey wr mawr, na gwreic da yn Iwerdon, e ymw(e)let a Branwen, ni rodei hi ae cae* ... *ydaw* (204–6), where *ni* ... *ydaw* is the negative form of the improper relative clause *y rodei hi ae cae* ... *ydaw*, and may be translated 'to whom she did not give' (cf. Sc. Gael. *nach [tug i] dhà*); *a mein sugyn yssyd ygwaelawt yr auon, ny eill na llong na llestyr arnei* (286–8); *a'r pump wraged hynny* ... *a anet udunt pum meib*

INTRODUCTION

(467-8). In this last instance *a* is the preverb, not the relative pronoun. This sentence is not relative in meaning; it is an example of the 'abnormal' sentence, as it is called in Mod. W.

Another example of lack of close articulation in a non-relative construction is *a'r penn a uyd kystal gennwch y gedymdeithas* (395-6), where there is a logical break after *penn*, and the poss. pron. *y* is used to provide the articulation.

Summary of the Scheme of the Four Branches, and the relationship of Branwen *to that scheme*

First Branch (*Pwyll*): When Pwyll, prince of Dyfed, is hunting he encounters Arawn king of Annwn, who asks for his help against a rival king Hafgan. Pwyll agrees to change form and place with Arawn for a year and a day. Pwyll goes to the court of Arawn, where his identity is unsuspected, and spends a year there in innocent enjoyment. At the end of a year and a day he keeps tryst with Hafgan, defeats him in single combat in the middle of a ford, and thereafter subdues Hafgan's kingdom. Then he meets Arawn, who expresses his gratitude to Pwyll, and they resume their own forms, and return to their respective homes. Arawn finds that Pwyll had been faithful to him in all things, their friendship is confirmed, and Pwyll is thereafter called 'Head of Annwn'.

Once, when sitting on the *gorsedd* or mound at Arberth, Pwyll sees a lovely maiden on a fine horse passing by, and after various attempts have been made to overtake her, Pwyll himself succeeds, and discovers that although she is pledged to marry another suitor, it is Pwyll she wishes to marry. They make a tryst for a year from that time. The maiden's name is Rhiannon, daughter of Hefeydd the Old.

At the wedding feast Rhiannon's former suitor, Gwawl son of Clud, asks a boon of Pwyll. This is granted and he asks for Rhiannon. She proposes a stratagem to Pwyll whereby Gwawl shall not win her, and a new tryst, between Rhiannon and Gwawl, is fixed. Rhiannon gives Pwyll a magical bag.

Pwyll comes in disguise to the feast, a year after the first feast, and asks for the fill of his bag, of food. The bag cannot be filled, and Rhiannon suggests that Gwawl should tread down the provisions in it. Pwyll takes the opportunity to close the bag on Gwawl; his hidden followers emerge and vanquish Gwawl's host, and they play at the game of 'Badger in the Bag', by striking the bag in which Gwawl is enclosed. Gwawl surrenders his claim to Rhiannon, and departs. The nuptials of Pwyll and Rhiannon are completed, and they depart to Arberth in Dyfed, where the nobles of Pwyll's country come to see them, and receive gifts from Rhiannon.

After two years Pwyll's subjects are perturbed because he has no heir, and they ask him to take another wife. Pwyll asks for a year's respite, and before the end of that time a son is born to Rhiannon. The boy is abducted on the night of his birth, and the women who should have kept watch smear Rhiannon with the blood of some pups which they have killed, and accuse her of murdering the child. Pwyll's leading subjects ask him to put away his wife. He does not agree to this, but a penance is imposed on her. She has to sit by a horse-block at the court of Arberth every day, tell her story to everyone who comes by, and offer to carry visitors into the court.

Teyrnon, lord of Gwent Is-Coed, had a handsome mare which foaled every May-eve, and on each occasion the colt disappeared. He keeps watch this May-eve, and sees the new-born colt being snatched at by a huge claw which came in at the window. He cuts off the arm from the elbow and saves the colt. On rushing out to chase the raider, he discovers a boy in swaddling clothes by the door. Teyrnon and his wife keep the boy, pretending that he is their own, and they call him Gwri Wallt Euryn. The boy prospers. The colt is later given to him as a gift.

Teyrnon and his wife hear of Rhiannon's mishap, and suspect that Gwri is Rhiannon's son, the more so as he closely resembles Pwyll. Teyrnon takes the boy to Arberth, and the lad refuses to be carried by Rhiannon. Gwri is welcomed at Pwyll's court, is restored to his family, and re-named Pryderi, on the instructions of Pendaran Dyfed, to whom he is given in fosterage.

Pwyll died eventually, and Pryderi ruled the seven cantrefs of Dyfed, and conquered the seven cantrefs of Seisyllwch. Then he took to wife Cigfa, a lady of noble descent.

Second Branch (*Branwen*): Bendigeidfran,[1] son of Llŷr, was

[1] In this summary, and in the succeeding discussion, the modern forms of Welsh names are used, as in the Everyman translation, by G. Jones and T. Jones, of the Mabinogion.

INTRODUCTION   xxiii

sitting on the rock of Harlech one day, in the company of his brother Manawydan, and his half-brothers Nisien and Efnisien, when they saw thirteen ships coming from Ireland. Bendigeidfran's men went down to meet them, and discovered that the ships belonged to Matholwch, king of Ireland, who had come to seek the hand of Branwen, daughter of Llŷr. It was decided to agree to the match, and the nuptials were to be celebrated at Aberffraw in Anglesey.

After the wedding-feast, Efnisien, who was of a quarrelsome nature, disfigured some of Matholwch's horses, and the Irish king decided to go away, smarting from this insult. Bendigeidfran tries to make peace, offering reparation, and he is successful in making Matholwch stay. In order to cement the friendship further, Bendigeidfran offers Matholwch a magical cauldron of regeneration which he had obtained from an Irishman, Llassar Llaes Gyfnewid, who had escaped from the Iron House in Ireland when it was set on fire. It transpires that Matholwch's council had arranged for this Iron House to be built to destroy Llassar and his family.

Matholwch and Branwen go to Ireland, where they are welcomed, and Branwen gives precious gifts to those who come to visit them. In due course a son, Gwern, is born, and he is put into fosterage. The following year there is a move to avenge the insult offered to Matholwch in Anglesey, and Branwen is made to suffer penance. She is compelled to cook in the court, and suffer daily buffets on the ear. An embargo is placed on traffic with Wales, so that Branwen's relatives will not hear of this, but after three years she evolves the plan of using a starling as a courier, and sends word to her brother. Bendigeidfran invades Ireland, leaving seven stewards (including Pendaran Dyfed, who was then a young lad) to guard his interests in Wales.

Bendigeidfran's marvellous appearance as he approaches Ireland is described to Matholwch. The Irish retreat beyond the river Shannon, destroying the bridge, but Bendigeidfran himself acts as a bridge. In an attempt to come to terms with him, the Irish build him a huge house (for he had never had one large enough to contain him). The Irish fasten two hundred hide bags to the pillars of the house, each bag having an armed man in it. Efnisien, who sees through this trick, crushes the skulls of the men in the bags. The Welsh and the Irish make peace in the house. Efnisien calls Gwern, who had been made king of Ireland, to him, and hurls him into the fire, so that he is burned to death. A battle breaks out, and for some time the Irish, by using the Cauldron of Regeneration, have the better of it. Efnisien succeeds in being thrown into the Cauldron, and bursts it. Thereafter the tide turns, but although the Welsh win the victory, only seven of them escape alive, among them being Pryderi and Manawydan. Bendigeidfran orders that his own head be struck off, and carried to the White Hill in London. He says that the seven men will be a long time on the road, will spend seven years at Harlech (where the birds of Rhiannon will sing to them), and will be four score years at Gwales in Penfro. They will stay there until they open the door facing Cornwall: then they must go to London to bury the head.

Branwen goes with the seven men, but she dies of a broken heart in Anglesey, and is buried there. As the seven proceed, they hear that Caswallawn son of Beli has been crowned king in London, and that the seven stewards left in charge by Bendigeidfran are dead. It appears that Pendaran Dyfed, who is again referred to as a boy, was additional to the seven, and he is said to have escaped. The survivors from Ireland spend the allotted time in Harlech and in Gwales, and finally have to go to London to bury Bendigeidfran's head.

Meantime five pregnant women had been left alive in Ireland. These give birth to five sons, and in due course the island is populated again, and divided into five provinces.

Third Branch (*Manawydan*): After the seven men, led by Manawydan and Pryderi, bury Bendigeidfran's head, Manawydan feels despondent. Pryderi bestows his mother Rhiannon on Manawydan, and with her, authority over the seven cantrefs of Dyfed. They return to Arberth in Dyfed, and the marriage takes place. Thereafter Pryderi and Cigfa, Manawydan and Rhiannon make a circuit of Dyfed.

Pryderi goes to Oxford to pay homage to Caswallawn, and after his return a feast is held at Arberth. The two couples go to the mound of Arberth, and a mist overtakes them. The court is desolate when they return, and the whole of Dyfed has become similarly uninhabited. For a year they hunt and fish, but then they grow weary of this, and Manawydan suggests that they go to England and seek some craft whereby they may make a living. They go to Hereford and Manawydan monopolizes the saddle trade there, incurring the wrath of the other saddlers. They move to another town and become shield-makers. A similar situation arises and they move on, this time becoming shoe-makers (Manawydan hopes that their shoemaker brethren will show a characteristic lack of spirit). Manawydan shows himself to be an excellent shoemaker also, the shoemakers plot against him, and the party returns to Dyfed.

One day Pryderi and Manawydan go out to hunt. In chasing a wild boar they come to a *caer* or fortress which had not existed in that part of the country before. The dogs follow the boar into the *caer*, and soon Pryderi, against Manawydan's advice, follows them. He finds neither boar nor dogs nor people in the *caer*, but he sees a golden bowl by the edge of a fountain; when he catches this in his hands he is transfixed, and loses power of movement and speech. Manawydan returns home and tells Rhiannon, who goes to seek Pryderi. The same fate befalls her. Then the *caer*, and with it Pryderi and Rhiannon, vanishes in thunder and mist.

Manawydan and Cigfa decide to return to England. Manawydan resumes his trade of shoemaker, but after a year the other shoemakers plot against him, and he and Cigfa return to Dyfed. Manawydan sows wheat, but when it ripens the ears disappear. He keeps watch one night, and discovers a huge host of mice stripping the stalks of wheat. He is able to catch one of the mice, a slow heavy one, and brings it home to hang. Cigfa advises him not to hang the mouse, and so does a clerk who comes past the mound of Arberth. Manawydan will not be persuaded. A priest then comes to plead for the mouse, and finally a bishop, with whom Manawydan drives a hard bargain. The mouse was in fact the bishop's pregnant wife, and in return for her freedom Manawydan secures the restoration of Pryderi and Rhiannon, the removal of the enchantment from Dyfed, and a promise of no reprisals from the bishop. The bishop was a friend of Gwawl son of Clud, Rhiannon's rejected suitor, and had laid the enchantment on Dyfed, and on Pryderi and Rhiannon, in revenge. Pryderi and Rhiannon are restored, and the enchantment is lifted off Dyfed. Rhiannon tells how she had been forced to have the asses' collars round her neck, as a punishment, when she was enchanted.

Fourth Branch (*Math*): Math, son of Mathonwy, was lord of Gwynedd, and Pryderi was lord of the seven cantrefs of Dyfed, the seven cantrefs of Morgannwg, the four of Ceredigiawn and the three of Ystrad Tywi. Math had a foot-bearer called Goewin, who had always to be with him. Gilfaethwy son of Dôn, Math's nephew, was in love with Goewin, and was wasting away for love of her. His brother Gwydion lays plans to help Gilfaethwy. He goes to Math and suggests that Pryderi be asked for the swine of Annwn (a present to Pwyll from Arawn). The brothers, along with ten others, go to Pryderi's court in the guise of bards. Gwydion charms the court with his tales, and asks Pryderi for the swine. Pryderi cannot give them until they have doubled their numbers in the country.

Gwydion makes, by means of magic, twelve stallions and twelve greyhounds, with saddles and bridles, collars and leashes of gold. These, together with twelve golden shields, are exchanged for the swine. But the spell under which these things were made lasts but one day, so Gwydion and his men hasten away with the swine, finally returning to Math's court. By this time Pryderi is mustering his forces, and Math does likewise, thus freeing Goewin from her duties to Math. Gilfaethwy and Goewin sleep together in Math's bed, against Goewin's will.

The next day the hosts of Pryderi and Math fight a battle, and Pryderi has to give twenty-four hostages to Math. Then Pryderi challenges Gwydion to single combat. With the aid of both strength and magic Gwydion kills Pryderi.

Math returns home to Caer Dathyl, and Goewin tells him of her rape by Gilfaethwy. Math promises redress, and says that he will make Goewin his wife.

When Gwydion and Gilfaethwy return to Caer Dathyl, Math strikes Gilfaethwy with his magic wand, and turns him into a hind. He turns Gwydion into a stag. They return in a year's time with a fawn of their breeding. Math turns the hind into a wild boar, and the stag into a wild sow, but he restores the fawn to the shape of a boy, and calls him Hyddwn. The boar and sow return in a year's time, with a young offspring. The parents are turned into wolves, and the offspring becomes a boy, Hychdwn. The offspring of the wolves next year is called Bleiddwn. Then Math restores Gwydion and Gilfaethwy to their human shapes.

Math asks their advice as to what maiden he should seek, and they suggest Aranrhod, Math's niece. She comes, and Math asks her to step over a wand as a test of her maidenhood. In doing this she drops a yellow-haired boy, and also something else, which Gwydion picks up, wraps in silk, and hides. The boy is baptized Dylan, and is later called Dylan Eil Ton (D. son of Wave).

Gwydion, who had hidden the other thing which Aranrhod

dropped, later discovers a baby boy in the silk wrappings, and he arranges for a nurse for the boy, who grows apace, becoming very large for his years. He follows Gwydion one day to Caer Aranrhod, and Aranrhod is discomfited on seeing him, and swears that the boy will not have a name until she gives him one. Gwydion goes away, makes a magic ship which he sails to Caer Aranrhod, and busies himself making shoes with beautifully wrought leather. Aranrhod asks him to make some for her, and before the transaction is completed she comes to the ship, and inadvertently gives the boy (her son and Gwydion's?) a name—Lleu Llaw Gyffes. Aranrhod then swears that the boy shall never take arms until she provides him with them.

The boy is reared by Gwydion. In due course he begins to long for arms, and he and Gwydion go in disguise to Caer Aranrhod, pretending to be bards from Morgannwg. Gwydion tells tales that evening. In the morning he creates by magic a sound of trumpets and mustering men, and a concourse of ships. He advises Aranrhod to defend the *caer*. She brings them arms, and so Aranrhod is again outwitted. She then swears that the boy shall never have a human wife.

Gwydion goes to Math, who suggests that a wife made of flowers be obtained for Lleu. This is done, and she is called Blodeuedd (i.e. 'Flowers').[1] Math also gives land to the boy.

Lleu goes to Math's court, and while he is away Blodeuedd falls in love with Gronw Pebyr, and they plot to slay Lleu. Blodeuedd discovers from Lleu, when he returns, how his death can be compassed, and she and Gronw make their preparations. Finally Lleu is struck, and flies away in the form of an eagle. The lovers are re-united. Math and Gwydion are sorely grieved by the news. Gwydion goes to search for Lleu, and finds him in the form of an eagle. He restores him to human form, but he is much emaciated. After a year's care from physicians he is whole again.

They go to seek Blodeuwedd.[2] Gwydion turns her into an owl, and makes all the other birds her enemies. Gronw Pebyr has to stand on the spot where Lleu stood when the spear was aimed at him, and Lleu kills him with a spear-cast. Lleu was lord thereafter over the land of Gwynedd. (*End of Summary*.)

---

[1] Ifor Williams (PKM 283) draws attention to other forms and interpretations of the name.

[2] This is the form used at this point in the story.

We may look first of all for evidence of connexion between the four branches, expecting from the title given to the series that they possess some kind of unity. Pryderi appears as a character in all four: in the first branch the circumstances of his birth are related; in the second, we have fleeting glimpses of him as one of the party which carried Bendigeidfran's head from Ireland to London; in the third, there is mention of his marriage and the bestowal of his mother in marriage to Manawydan, to whom he plays a largely subordinate role; in the fourth, he is the leader of the party opposed to Math, and meets his death early in this branch of the story. He has thus some formal claim to be regarded as the central character of the story: the episodes observe a proper temporal sequence from birth, through boyhood, to marriage, adult action, and finally death. In the case of no other character does the tale give evidence of a similar development. If, however, we are to regard him as the hero, his case is not analogous to that of a hero of classical or of Irish stories—his role is too episodic. Two solutions of this difficulty are possible: (1) the original pattern of a Pryderi saga has been overgrown and obscured, or (2) the pattern of a Pryderi saga has been imposed on other, earlier material. The first of these solutions has been more generally adopted. The fundamental pattern of the Four Branches has been seen as identical with the Irish pattern of *compert-macgnimartha-tochmarc* or *indarba-aided*. (The third branch contains in reality the marriage, not the wooing, and Pryderi's imprisonment and rescue play a larger part in the branch than his marriage does. The marriage had also been mentioned at the end of the first branch.) If this is the case, the survival of the pattern seems almost fortuitous, especially with regard to the second and fourth branches, and it is perhaps as easy to believe that the final redactor, or at any rate an eleventh-century redactor, has imposed this pattern on otherwise loosely connected tales with a perfunctoriness of which we can find other evidence.

It is beyond doubt that this redactor considered the four branches as part of the one work. The beginning of the third branch is linked with the second branch by a reference to 'the seven men of whom we spoke above' (. . . [*y*] *seithwyr a dywedyssam ni uchot*). Here also there is a link with the end of the first branch, in the reference to the seven cantrefs of Dyfed to which Pryderi had succeeded, and the opening of the fourth branch reinforces the link with a similar reference to the seven cantrefs, and another to the four cantrefs of Ceredigiawn and the three of Ystrad Tywi which Pryderi is said, at the end of the first branch, to have conquered. Many of the characters appear, or are referred to, in more than one of the branches e.g. Rhiannon, Arawn, Pwyll, Gwawl son of Clud, Cigfa, Manawydan, Pendaran Dyfed, Llassar Llaes Gyfnewid, Caswallawn. Dyfed (and especially Arberth) is the scene of much of the action in the first and third branches, but the main interest in the fourth branch switches to Gwynedd, and the second branch does not seem to be connected with Dyfed at all.[1] On the other hand, the consistency of the tale as a whole is by no means rigorous. Pendaran Dyfed appears as Pryderi's foster-father in the first branch, but in the second he is twice described as a young lad.[2] Similarly, Pryderi's role, as one of the seven men who went to London, seems to have changed between the second branch, where he is scarcely mentioned, and the third, where he initially seems to have been joint leader with Manawydan, but later plays second fiddle to him.

Pryderi's part is not central to the action of any one branch of the tale. It gives, however, to the whole a unity which may be underlying or overlaid.

The complexity of the Four Branches is remarkable, and the stories and myths which underlie the extant text have been

[1] As was shown by Anwyl (ZCP ii, 124–7), the second and fourth branches, and particularly the fourth, are much more circumstantial than the first and third in their enumeration of place-names.

[2] ll. 248, 423–4.

brilliantly and ingeniously analysed by the late Prof. W. J. Gruffydd in his two books *Math vab Mathonwy* and *Rhiannon*. The complex would appear to be one of immemorial myths and heroic tales, influenced by historical traditions, and finally welded and moulded by an editor[1] who may well have been a cleric whose moralistic and satirical tendencies are generally, but not always, submerged by his ambition to tell a good story well. It is evident that this redactor, like many of his predecessors who passed on individual tales, was, in Matthew Arnold's phrase, 'pillaging an antiquity of which he did not fully possess the secret'. Thus, Gruffydd in *Rhiannon* argued convincingly that the episodes concerning Rhiannon in the first and third branches preserve fragments of a myth of a British *Rīgantona* or 'Great Queen' who became identified with the Horse Goddess *Epona*. Rhiannon, Teyrnon, and Gwri/Gweir would have stood in this myth in the relationship of mother, father, and son. Again, Gruffydd argued that Manawydan, in the third branch, is in origin the Irish sea-god Manannan Mac Lir, although his character is greatly changed in the Welsh story.[2] This, Gruffydd suggested,[3] may be due to a clerical author superimposing notions of chastity and chivalry on a character who was singularly ill-fitted to be an exemplar of these virtues. This theme is further developed by Mrs. N. K. Chadwick in her paper 'Literary Tradition in the Old Norse and Celtic World'.[4] Folklore motifs, as that of the *Demon Hand*, and the *Faithful Dog*, at one time became attached to the central story, and in turn became partially detached from it, and the theme of the *Calumniated Wife* assumed considerable importance in the first and second branches (the wives being Rhiannon and Branwen).[5] Myths concerning the King of the Otherworld were

[1] It need not be assumed that this 'editor' was also the author of *Branwen*.
[2] For a useful discussion of this point, see Mac Cana 122–9.
[3] *Rhiannon* 78.
[4] *Saga-Book*, xiv, part 3.
[5] See *Rhiannon* 60 ff.

brought into association with traditions of the province of Dyfed, fragmenting and almost submerging these traditions. It has further been suggested that the final redactor of the Four Branches was himself a Dyfed man, and attempted to codify the chief tales of the various Welsh kingdoms, much as their Laws had been codified, but approximately a century later.[1]

Other investigations have sought to establish the identity of certain characters in the Four Branches with characters in Arthurian Romance as it reappears on the Continent. Thus R. S. Loomis identifies the Fisher King Bron in the Grail Cycle with Brân (or Bendigeidfran), and both with Lugh and Manannán in Irish tradition. He suggests that Pryderi may be identified with Perceval, and Gwri (Pryderi's *alter ego*) with Bors and also with Gawain.[2]

Loomis argued, further, that much of the story of *Branwen*, particularly the second part, which may originally have been a separate story,[3] reappears in the late thirteenth-century French poem *Sone de Nausay*.[4] In this poem Joseph of Arimathea has taken the place of the Fisher King, elsewhere called Bron. Both the Fisher King and Brân had connexions with England (*Lloegr* in Welsh, *Lorgres* in the French poem); both led a victorious expedition to a foreign land; Brân was wounded in the foot, the Fisher King in the reins and below, and thereafter Britain in the one case and England in the other became a Waste Land; Brân ordained that after his death his followers should dwell for eighty years on an island off the coast of Wales, and the Fisher King founded a community which after his death occupied an island castle called Galoche, i.e. Welsh; the followers of both feasted without stint in an enclosed place overlooking the sea; Brân's followers preserved his head on an island off the coast

---

[1] PKM xxxix–xl. Mac Cana, 181–7, makes the tentative suggestion that this redactor was Rhigyfarch, or his father Sulien, bishop of St. David's (†1091), or both in collaboration.
[2] WAL 35.   [3] Gruffydd, Cymm. Trans. 1912–13, p. 56.
[4] WAL, chap. iv.

of Wales, and the Fisher King's community preserved his body in the island castle of Galoche.[1]

With regard to *Branwen*, W. J. Gruffydd, adumbrating a study which had unfortunately not been completed at the time of his death, suggested that the original central theme of the second branch was a raid on Annwn by Pryderi: '... *Branwen* contains, hidden under the surface, a garbled account of (Pryderi's) traditionally great feat, namely the Expedition to the Other-world, and his snatching from Pen Annwvn, the chief of the Other-world, his Cauldron of Resurrection.'[2]

---

[1] Summarized from op. cit. 56–57. Mac Cana, in his discussion of Mordwyt Tyllyon (162–5) supports the identification of Brân with the Fisher King. See l. 371 n.

For the notion of Brân as a patron of seafarers and of fishermen, for speculations on the origin of his name, and for parallels, in other literatures, to aspects of his character, see A. H. Krappe's interesting article in *Études Celtiques* iii, 27–37.

[2] *Rhiannon* 11. Gruffydd had been of this opinion in 1939 according to a letter quoted in WAL 60 n. where he said: 'I have no doubt that the attack on Ireland in *Branwen* is to be traced to an attack on Annwfn for the possession of the *Pair*.' Gruffydd's views are further defined in an article by A. O. H. Jarman in *Llên Cymru* iv, 129–34.

It is reasonably certain that the story of the *pair* and that of the Iron House are not essentially connected. Stories of magic cauldrons were no doubt associated with Ireland by the Welsh *cyfarwyddiaid* or story-tellers (cf. the tale of the cauldron of Diwrnach the Irishman in *Kulhwch ac Olwen*, IEW 202). The five *bruidne* mentioned in *Scéla Mucce Meic Da Thó* have each a cauldron which can supply an unending quantity of food, but although these *bruidne* are said to be located in Ireland they may well be mythological in origin, and belong to the Otherworld (see EIHM 122). The *pair dadeni* in *Branwen* seems to have some of the characteristics of a cornucopia, so that it is perhaps more than a coincidence that Tudur Aled mentions both the *pair* and the *corn* together:

'... A rhoi Pair Tyrnog i'r côg a'r cigydd,
    A Chorn Brân Galed, trai yfed trefydd ...' (GTA i. 23).

Is it possible that in the earlier mythical story the swine of Annwn (to be compared perhaps with the pigs of Manannán) were cooked in this cauldron, magically revived, and eaten over and over again? Is it possible also to see a connexion between the ruffianly Llassar, who is accompanied by his ugly wife, and the *bachlach* Fer Caille with the

The story of a *pair dadeni*, or Cauldron of Resurrection, forms, of course, an important part of the second branch, entering into the narrative at various points.[1] If we accept the suggestion that Pryderi is the central character of the Four Branches, and that the second branch, on the Irish analogy, should consist of his *macgnimartha* or Youthful Exploits, then Gruffydd's reconstruction is more than plausible. If this argument should be accepted, it would support the thesis that the original pattern of a Pryderi saga has been overgrown rather than that it has been superimposed on other material.

External Influences on Branwen

The presence in the Four Branches of folklore motifs which have wide ramifications in the literature, particularly the folk-literature, of other countries has been mentioned in the preceding section. Certain closer connexions, which imply borrowing in one direction or another, have been discerned in the Mabinogi, and particularly in the story of *Branwen*. Timothy Lewis, in his *Mabinogi Cymru*, made an eccentric and misguided attempt to show that these tales were basically of Norse origin. His distortion of the evidence and his special pleading make it impossible to accept his thesis. A more tentative, and much more convincing, approach to this problem has been made by Mrs. Chadwick in her article on 'Literary Tradition in the Old Norse and Celtic World'. Here it is suggested, for example, that there is a close connexion between the story of Pwyll and Arawn in the first branch, and the Norse *Saga of Egill and Ásmundr*, in which the prince Ásmundr meets a supernatural huntsman Arán, and makes a 'strange compact to spend a stated period of time in the supernatural regions'.[2] The similarity in the names, Arawn and Arán, which seem to be

unprepossessing woman in *Togail Bruidne Da Derga*? Is Llassar, like Fer Caille, in origin the lord of the feast in the Otherworld *bruiden*? (Mac Cana, 39-44, gives detailed reasons for connecting Llassar and Fer Caille.)   [1] See ll. 139, 375.   [2] *Saga Book* xiv 175.

unknown elsewhere in Welsh and Norse literature, and in the circumstances, is striking, and Mrs. Chadwick suggests that the saga may originally have been a Hebridean one.[1] It could have passed from the Hebrides directly to Ireland, and to Wales either directly or through an Irish intermediary.

The evidence of direct borrowing from Irish sources is both more extensive and more conclusive. The evidence afforded by style and plot construction will be discussed later. Here various incidental indications of Irish influence may be listed, and one or two important borrowings discussed in detail. The telling of onomastic stories, as that of Branwen's grave by the Alaw,[2] is a favourite device in the Irish sagas, the most famous and sustained example being the *Acallamh na Senórach* (although this is in fact later in date).[3] Ifor Williams[4] saw in the use of *Llinon*, for the Irish river Shannon, evidence of an oral rather than a literary loan from Irish. In the incident of Bendigeidfran acting as a bridge over the river, and having hurdles placed over him,[5] W. J. Gruffydd saw a hidden reference to and an explanation of the name which Dublin has in Mod. Ir.: *Baile Átha Cliath* 'The Town of the Ford of the Hurdles'. Proinsias Mac Cana thinks that Gruffydd was completely justified in this, and concludes that the name suggested to the author of *Branwen* the Shannon-bridging episode. Proposing an emendation of the text at l. 290 (see note), he goes on to suggest that the author of *Branwen* shows a good knowledge of Irish geography.[6]

An instance of Irish influence of a different type is the story of the Irishman Llassar.[7] Bendigeidfran tells how Llassar and his companions/descendants were settled in various parts of

---

[1] A somewhat similar suggestion is made by Mrs. Chadwick regarding the stories of Manannán and Manawydan, in SGS viii, 115.

[2] l. 409.

[3] Cf., however, the Irish eleventh-century *Cóir Anmann*, 'Fitness of Names'. [4] PKM 196. [5] l. 296. [6] Mac Cana 117–21.

[7] ll. 150 ff. On the question of borrowed elements in this story, see op. cit. 39 ff.

Wales, and how they prospered there. The reference is probably to the historical Irish settlements in Wales, and may be an onomastic story designed to explain the presence of place-names containing the element 'Gwyddel', e.g. Gwyddelwern, &c. Cecile O'Rahilly suggested that the circumstances of the expulsion of the Déssi, and their subsequent fortunes in Dyfed, tally in broad outline with those of Llassar.[1]

Again, the story of the five pregnant women who survived in Ireland, and whose descendants populated the five divisions or provinces of Ireland (*pymp rann Ywerdon*),[2] seems to show that the author of the story was familiar with the Irish word *cóiced* ('a fifth' developing the sense of 'a province') and its meaning. Mac Cana (32-37) goes a good deal further, and argues that the author of *Branwen* was familiar with the legend of the revolt of the *Aithechthuatha*, a legend which appears in (1) *Lebor Gabála*, according to which the widow of Fiachu Findolad fled to Alba and 'gave birth to Tuathal, who returned twenty years after to reconquer Ireland', and (2) the story of Cairbre Cattchenn, in which it is related how Cairbre, 'who belonged to the *aithechthuatha*, slew the *soerchlanda* (i.e. the free or noble peoples i.e. the Goidels), and how three of their wives, who were pregnant, escaped to Alba and gave birth to sons. Meanwhile the crops and produce failed in Ireland . . . and at length the three exiled princes were recalled. . . . After their return they became kings of Tara, Munster and Ulster, and thus it is from them that the free peoples of Ireland, the Goidels, take their descent.' Mac Cana goes on to point out that when the author of *Branwen* may be assumed to have been at work on the story, 'the well established Irish view was that the main incident in *Togail Bruidne Da Derga*, the death of Conaire Mór, brought about a period of rule by five provincial kings representing the five provinces. Similarly in *Branwen* the fight at the house in Ireland leads to the division of the country into

[1] *Ireland and Wales*, 106, n. 1.   [2] l. 474.

five provinces ruled by five provincial kings.' As Mac Cana shows fairly conclusively in other instances that the author of *Branwen* was familiar with the story of *Togail Bruidne Da Derga*,[1] his argument here is convincing.

Although perhaps not due to direct borrowing, it may be worth noting that the marvellous powers of the Birds of Rhiannon[2] are paralleled in Irish literature: e.g. in the story of *Aislinge Óenguso*,[3] Óengus and Caer assume the shape of white birds and go to Brug Maicc in Óicc where they sing in musical harmony, putting the people there to sleep for three days and three nights.[4]

One of the most remarkable examples in *Branwen* of borrowing from Irish sources, and one of the most conclusive, is the incident of the iron house which was set on fire with the intention of destroying Llassar Llaes Gyfnewid and his wife and child. There are various accounts of similar episodes in Irish literature,[5] as in the story of *Orgain Denna Ríg* ('The Destruction of Dinn Ríg'),[6] a ninth- or tenth-century text. In this case the house is made entirely of iron. Thrice fifty smith's bellows are set around the house, with four warriors at each bellows. Over 700 men are said to have perished in this house. A house-burning episode is much less elaborately recorded in the *Bóroma*,[7] which belongs to the tenth or eleventh century. An entry in the Annals of Ulster, s.a. 1046, records the burning of Muiredach son of Flaithbertach Hua Néill in a house set on

---

[1] See especially Mac Cana 24–31, 39–50, and 87–93. In the last of these discussions the instances are necessarily more tentative, but the cumulative sum of such instances is impressive.

[2] l. 395.   [3] Ed. F. Shaw, 63.

[4] Mac Cana (102–9) discusses other instances also.

[5] See *Ireland and Wales*. Burnings of houses are frequently mentioned in the Norse sagas also. See A. W. Johnston, 'Some Medieval House-burnings by the Vikings of Orkney', *Sc. Hist. Review* xii, 157–65.

[6] ZCP iii, 1–14. A recent ed. is that of David Greene, in *Fingal Rónáin* 16–26. Greene is of the opinion that the iron house incident is a later addition to this tenth-century story.   [7] Stokes, *RC* xiii, 61.

fire by Cú Ulad son of Congalach, and C. O'Rahilly suggests[1] that this incident may have been fresh news in Wales at the time when the tale of *Branwen* assumed its present form. Even if this suggestion implies too early a dating for *Branwen*, it may be worth noting.

But the Irish account to which that in *Branwen* is most closely parallel is in the Irish tale *Mesca Ulad*. Certain difficulties arise here, which make it impossible to say that the account of the episode in *Branwen* was directly borrowed from any extant Irish text. The two main versions of *Mesca Ulad* are those contained in *Lebor na hUidre* (in a section written *c.* A.D. 1100) and in the *Book of Leinster* (*c.* A.D. 1160). Neither text is complete, and there is a section where the two overlap. This section concerns in part the references to the iron house, and the *Book of Leinster* version is clearly an expansion of the *Lebor na hUidre* one, and is due to the later redactor.[2] J. C. Watson doubted if the earlier version had contained any extended description of the preparation of the iron house. What are we to conclude from this evidence? Hardly that the borrowing of the description is from Welsh into Irish. The recurrence of the theme in Irish literature makes this unlikely. It is even harder to accept the possibility of both accounts deriving, as Loth suggested, from an original community of myth.[3] The resemblances in the two accounts are too circumstantial to admit explanation by coincidence. It may clarify the issue to tabulate parallel elements in the accounts given in *Branwen* and in *Mesca Ulad*.

Branwen	*Mesca Ulad*
1. Llassar Llaes Gyfnewid and his wife had made a nuisance of themselves.	1. The Ulstermen had wandered in a drunken orgy into Connacht, the territory of their enemies.

[1] *Ireland and Wales* 107 n.
[2] See J. C. Watson, *Mesca Ulad*, xvii–xviii, and *Ériu* xiii, 111.
[3] RC xi, 347.

2. Matholwch's council decides to build a house of iron. Charcoal is piled as high as the top of the chamber.

3. Every smith in Ireland was summoned, those who had tongs and hammers.

4. Llassar and his wife and offspring were served with ample meat and drink.

5. When they were intoxicated, the charcoal was set alight, and the bellows applied until the house was white-hot.

6. When the wall is white-hot, Llassar charges it with his shoulder, and breaks out, together with his wife. No one else escapes. But later it appears that a considerable number came to Wales from Ireland along with Llassar, as they are quartered throughout the country.

2. The coming of the Ulstermen had been prophesied, and a house of iron, with inner and outer layers of board, and an earthen house below filled with firewood and coal, had been prepared for them.

3. Thrice fifty smiths were summoned.

4. Choice portions of food and drink were served to the Ulstermen.

5. The Ulstermen were intoxicated. The smiths had brought bellows with them. The Ulstermen feel the fierce heat of the fire from below and from above.

6. Cú Chulainn says that he will do with his sword *Cruadín* a deed by which all the men of Ulster shall go out (from the house). He then thrusts his sword to the hilt through the three walls of the house, thus discovering that the interior wall is made of iron. The next part of the story is missing, but we find Cú Chulainn and the Ulstermen at large afterwards.

We may perhaps surmise that the accounts given in *Branwen* and in *Mesca Ulad* bear a close relation to a third, unidentified, account which combined elements of both descriptions. In this third account the house may have been made simply of iron, as in *Branwen* and *Orgain Denna Ríg*, and we may assume that the smiths were summoned in the first instance to build the house (hence the reference, otherwise meaningless, to tongs and hammers in *Branwen*). A large company was feasted, to the point of intoxication, in the house. A chamber below the house had already been filled with inflammable material (firewood and charcoal), and while the feast was proceeding, similar materials were piled roof-high outside the house. When the appropriate moment came, the doors of the house were made fast and the fire was started, both in the subterranean chamber and outside, and thrice fifty bellows were operated by a large number of smiths, so that the inmates soon felt the fierce heat *from below and from above*. (The *Mesca Ulad* account has no reference to the piling of charcoal, &c., outside the walls, but the reference to *from above*, makes it clear that this had been done. Conversely, the *Branwen* account makes no mention of the subterranean chamber.) The leader of the trapped company made a breach in the wall, and led out the whole or part of his band. In *Branwen* we are at first given to understand that only Llassar, his wife, and his child (whose age cannot well be determined, as the reading *pedwyryd mis* from R almost certainly requires emendation; but since *plant* is used, a tender age is implied) were in the house. However, the phrase *a neb ny dieghis odyna namyn ef a'e wreic* ('and no one escaped thence except him(self) and his wife') suggests a larger number than three for the trapped company. This interpretation is further supported by the reference to the people (logically followers or companions of Llassar) who were quartered 'in every part of the kingdom' when Llassar arrived in Wales. We may perhaps surmise that Llassar and his Cauldron do not properly belong to the Iron House story at all; that since the author of *Branwen* wishes to spotlight Llassar he eliminates for the time being the larger company which was traditionally trapped in the Iron House; and that he allows them to slip back into the story at the end of his account, influenced by his desire to give a plausible explanation of the Irish colonies and place-names in Wales. Such an explanation would not be unjust to the author of *Branwen*, or its final redactor, who did not care specially for the tying-up of loose ends and the forging of a logical, streamlined plot. It may be said in extenuation, however, that the story of the Iron House is largely incidental to the story of *Branwen*, and the author may for this reason have taken less care with its details.

In view of the fact that the version of the Iron House story which is closest to that of *Branwen* is in the manuscript of *c.* 1160 rather than in that of *c.* 1100, there is the possibility that the version in *Branwen* may be an interpolation, later than the main redaction of the Four Branches.[1]

Humorous and fantastical exaggeration is a feature of many of the Irish sagas, particularly of the Middle Irish tales; this exaggeration is carried over into Irish and Scottish Gaelic folktales, and appears even in such late poetry as the eighteenth-century Alasdair Mac Mhaighstir Alasdair's *Birlinn Chlainn Raghnaill*. There is one descriptive passage in particular in *Branwen* which seems to show the influence of this tradition—the description, and Branwen's interpretation of that description, of Bendigeidfran's approach to Ireland. It is also a favourite device in Irish stories to stage a dramatic conversation of this type, in which the watchers of an approaching enemy, or hostile band, discuss the enemy's identity. The passage in *Branwen* occurs at ll. 258 ff., and may be paraphrased:

Matholwch's swineherds were by the sea one day, and they saw a strange sight on the sea. They came to report to Matholwch that they had seen a wood or forest on the sea, where they had never before seen a single tree. They saw also a large mountain, in motion, beside the wood. The mountain had a high ridge, with a lake on each side of it. Matholwch decides that if anyone can interpret this description Branwen can. She does so with

[1] See also Mac Cana's discussion of the Iron House story at pp. 16–23 of his book.

INTRODUCTION

ease: these are the men of the Island of the Mighty; the forest is composed of the masts and yard-arms of their ships. The mountain is Bendigeidfran, the ridge is his nose, and the two lakes are his eyes, one on each side of his nose.

The original dramatic purpose of such descriptions of approaching enemies is overlaid here by the humorous purpose, and a curious combination of dramatic tension and light relief is achieved. This combination can be paralleled in Irish literature, as in the description, in *Togail Bruidne Da Derga*, of Mac Cécht,[1] of which the following is the part which most closely resembles the passage in *Branwen*:

In dias mael im an ḟer co folt at-chondarcasiu, it é a dá glún ima chend. In dá loch im śliab ad-chondarcaisi, it é a dí śúil ima śróin. (The two bald ones that you have seen on either side of the man with hair, these are his knees on either side of his head. The two lakes you have seen on either side of a mountain, these are his eyes on either side of his nose.)

Togail Bruidne Da Derga contains a series of descriptions, the above quotation being only a small portion of one such.

Proinsias Mac Cana, in a highly convincing discussion of this passage in *Branwen*,[2] makes it clear that *Togail Bruidne Da Derga* was the source. In the Irish text Mac Cécht is described as lying down. The fantastic description of the nose and eyes makes sense in such a context, but not in the context in *Branwen*, where Bendigeidfran is *walking upright*. The Welsh author has also added the description of the ships, and of Bendigeidfran's mountainous body. Mac Cana also suggests that the swineherds of Matholwch derive from the swineherd of Maine Milscothach in *Togail Bruidne Da Derga*, and that the name Matholwch may have been suggested by the Irish name Milscothach.[3]

Eleanor Knott, quoting Thurneysen's analysis of *Togail*

---

[1] C. O'Rahilly drew attention to this. See *Ireland and Wales* 109.
[2] Mac Cana 24–32.
[3] The argument for this identification is not strong.

Bruidne Da Derga, says: 'the transmitted version, the work of the Compiler, which is represented by the Yellow Book of Lecan copy, was compiled in the eleventh century from two versions of a floating tradition, which were written down probably in the ninth century.'[1] It would seem, then, that the redactor or author of *Branwen* is here drawing on a tradition which was firmly established in Ireland by the eleventh century.

Another passage in which the author of *Branwen* may have been influenced by *Togail Bruidne Da Derga* is that in which he tells how the head of Bendigeidfran provided pleasant company and entertainment for eighty years in Gwales.[2] In *Togail Bruidne Da Derga* the severed head of Conaire 'utters verses of gratitude and praise' to Mac Cécht.[3] Also, in the Irish tale *Cath Almaine*, the head of Donn Bó sings 'so sweetly that all the company wept at the sadness of the music that it sang'.[4]

Finally, it has been suggested by Proinsias Mac Cana that the character of Efnisien has been modelled closely on that of Bricriu Nemthenga, who appears as a minor character in many of the tales of the Ulster cycle, and as the central character in *Fled Bricrenn*. This may be readily accepted, especially as Mac Cana finds other similarities between *Branwen* and *Fled Bricrenn*.[5]

Literary Quality and Style of Branwen

Branwen might well be described as a novel compressed to the dimensions of a short story. It is a story which constantly retains its interest, by means both of plot construction and of character delineation. These main qualities of the tale are never subordinated to the incidental antiquarian tricks and trappings which the average story-teller of this period would

[1] E. Knott, *Togail Bruidne Da Derga* xi.
[2] ll. 441 ff.   [3] Mac Cana 93.
[4] See Dillon, *The Cycles of the Kings* 99–102, where the parallel is noted.
[5] See Mac Cana 78–84 and also 28, 43–44, 72, and 141–2.

probably have found difficult to control. But the redactor is true to his time and to his class in that he does not entirely expunge these trappings from his story. The plot is carefully set: the main characters are introduced, and the main purpose of Matholwch's visit to Wales—to ask for the hand of Branwen—is made clear. The treatment is generally a dramatic one. We see the thirteen ships approaching from the south of Ireland, and their movement and appearance are described (13-22). The curiosity of the watchers on the shore is vividly suggested. The same technique is used with a greater wealth of detail in the description of Bendigeidfran's approach to Ireland (258-81). The contretemps between Matholwch and Bendigeidfran over the maiming of the horses is handled with great skill throughout its various stages: Matholwch's genuine puzzlement; the shifting of the action back and forth between the two parties, whose discussions are in turn reported; the gradual reconciliation, finally effected over the banquet by the two main characters; the friendly exchange of stories about Llassar and the *Pair Dadeni* or Cauldron of Resurrection. Later, when the tables are neatly turned, and it is Bendigeidfran's turn to feel aggrieved (over the treatment of Branwen in Ireland), there is a similar anxious consultation, but this time the anxiety is mainly on Matholwch's side. The story is now being told very much from the Welsh angle. Again, the episode after the Irish reconciliation, which is rudely shattered by the throwing of Gwern into the fire, is told with a fine sense of dramatic timing.

There is an element of balance in the construction of the plot: the approach to Wales at the beginning is contrasted with that to Ireland in the second half of the story; each side is insulted, and after negotiation appeased; the main protagonists are kings, one of Ireland and the other of the Island of the Mighty, and the action moves with a stately rhythm from one country to the other.

The delineation of character is well controlled. On one

occasion the sharp contrast between two characters is stated, in the case of Nisien and Efnisien (and this contrast is perhaps implied in the very names, by the prefix to the latter making it the negative or opposite of the former). Efnisien acts in character throughout, maliciously and systematically frustrating the ruse of the Irish (331-49), and treacherously throwing Gwern into the fire (361-6). But his actions may be governed not only by his mischievous disposition, but also by his intense loyalty to Ynys y Kedyrn (cf. 380-1). Sometimes character is suggested by physical description, as in the case of Llassar (158-60). The magician-like character of Bendigeidfran may have been imposed on him by a mythological origin, but apart from this the main impression he makes is one of strength—he is the champion *par excellence* of Ynys y Kedyrn, as Matholwch is (with the dice loaded against him) of Ireland. Branwen, perhaps like many other women in the age and circle of Gruffydd ap Cynan, has divided loyalties, and her character, moreover, is not inconsistent with a thoroughly Christian *milieu*, and may well have taken its shape in the mind of a clerical redactor.

However that may be, the story unfolds against a heroic background, in which pre-ordained forces work relentlessly towards a tragic dénouement. Treachery, death, and destruction are the sequel to a short period of romantic bliss; Heilyn cannot but open the door looking towards Cornwall, and thus bring to an end, as had been prophesied, the felicity of the eighty-year sojourn in Gwales. Even when Bendigeidfran's head is buried in London, the respite will be only a temporary one, for the head will be exhumed, and oppression will fall on Ynys y Kedyrn. It is almost as though the redactor of this tale shared the defeatism and pessimism which Matthew Arnold attributed, not entirely without reason, to the Celts.

The traditional and the personal artistry of the story-teller may be seen in many touches. The onomastic element has been mentioned above. There are the conventional enumerations, as of the names of messengers (89 and 109–10), of the seven who were left as stewards of Ynys y Kedyrn (245–8), of the seven men who escaped (388–90). There are several triadic groupings, used perhaps to lend historical authority, as well as dramatic force, as in ll. 45–46, 95–96, 422–3, 461–2, and 478.[1] There is much less than is usual, particularly in Irish tales, of the repetition of a theme or formula, but examples do occur, as when Efnisien squeezes the heads of the Irish warriors in the bags (334–49); descriptions of feasts proceed by formula at times, with the seating arrangements described (52–55), and then the steady pleasant progress of the feast, followed by sleep (58–60, 197–9).

The syntax of Medieval Welsh, like that of Irish and Scottish Gaelic, does not easily lend itself to the composition of flowing periods, in which clauses are articulated by a pleasing variety of syntactical devices. It is not uncommon in the prose of these languages to find the conjunction for 'and' used extensively to link clauses and to open sentences. The prose of *Branwen* is no exception. Where the author wishes to achieve variety in this respect, as sometimes, apparently, he does, it is generally by altering the normal word-order of the sentence, and bringing forward the subject, or by introducing the sentence with a *sef* construction. This, together with the greater variety which is natural to dialogue, breaks what might otherwise have become monotony. The dialogue is natural and free in its movement, and is often conducted with a swift-moving economy and terseness. But there is time for humour, and for revealing characterization, as when Branwen, addressed as 'arglwydes' ('lady'), prefaces her reply with 'Kyn ny bwyf arglwydes' ('though I may not be a lady') (271). Indeed, great care would seem to have been taken with the dialogue, which is

---

[1] W. J. Gruffydd, in 'The Mabinogion' (*Cymm.* 1912–13, 58) argues that the greater frequency of triads in *Branwen* suggests that this branch is less ancient than *Pwyll*.

always in keeping with the character of the speaker, whether it be the solicitous Bendigeidfran, trying to regain Matholwch's confidence, or the imperious Bendigeidfran, taking upon himself the responsibilities of the leader, and saying that he will act as a bridge; Efnisien in sardonic and laconic mood, pressing to pulp the heads of Irish warriors, or with a mixture of evil contemplation and incipient remorse deciding to throw the boy Gwern headlong into the fire.

More individual artistic touches may be noticed, as where the starling sent by Branwen as a messenger alights on Bendigeidfran's shoulder, and *ruffles its feathers*, thus disclosing the letter Branwen had sent to her brother. Sensitively handled also are the dramatically affecting passages where Bendigeidfran gives instructions to his followers as to where to carry his severed head (391–402), and the passages near the end of the story, describing the sojourn in Harlech (425–32), the stay in Gwales (434–48), and the dejection which the small band suffered once the door looking towards Cornwall was opened. These passages are among the most notable in the Four Branches, and they show us a writer perfectly attuned to his subject-matter, immersed in the emotions of his characters, moulding his phrases and shaping the rhythm of his sentences with assured and ripe artistry.[1]

Composition of the Text

As diplomatic texts from the White Book and Red Book are available, I have not considered it necessary to give all the textual variants. I have given a representative selection of variants which concern only orthographical differences, and these differences are more fully discussed in the section on orthography above. Variants other than orthographical ones are exhaustively quoted. Where I have adopted an earlier editorial emendation (as from I. W.'s ed. of the *Pedeir Keinc*)

[1] For further comment on the literary style of *Branwen*, see Mac Cana 177–80.

this is given within brackets (see ll. 65, 113, 131, 157, 224, 426–7, 458, 482) and I have given the readings of both W and R in the footnotes. Similarly, words supplied from R are printed within brackets in the text at ll. 170, 461. In two instances (ll. 285 and 448) brackets are used editorially, to indicate that a phrase, and a sentence, are in parenthesis. Apart from these instances noted above, the text is that of W throughout. Where the reading of R is probably or clearly better, this is indicated by *sic leg.?* or *sic leg.* after the appropriate variant reading (ll. 30, 107, 153, 166, 262, 264, 337, 453).

Except where the contrary is stated, variants given in the footnotes are from the Red Book. The entire passage from Peniarth 6, corresponding to ll. 293–342 of our text, is printed on pp. 42–43, although the main variants from P have been incorporated in the footnotes. Some discussion of the forms of P is given in the section on orthography.

The orthographical forms of the manuscript sources are preserved throughout. Words are generally separated, however, according to modern usage, the apostrophe is supplied in *a'r, y'r, o'r*, &c., and capitals, punctuation, and paragraphing are similarly supplied.

BIBLIOGRAPHY

(Books and manuscripts referred to in the text)

Acal.	*Acallamh na Senórach*, ed. W. Stokes (Leipzig, 1900).
	Aislinge Óenguso, ed. F. Shaw (Dublin, 1934).
	Bàrdachd Ghàidhlig, ed. W. J. Watson (3rd ed., Glasgow, 1959).
Bull.	*Bulletin of the Board of Celtic Studies* (Cardiff, 1921–).
Cymm.	*Y Cymmrodor* (London, 1877–).
Cymm. Trans.	*Transactions of the Honourable Society of Cymmrodorion* (London 1892–3–).
	Myles Dillon, *The Cycles of the Kings* (London, 1946).
EIHM	T. F. O'Rahilly, *Early Irish History and Mythology* (Dublin, 1946).
	Ériu (Dublin, 1904–).
	Fingal Rónáin and other stories, ed. David Greene (Dublin, 1955).
	Gaelic Songs of Mary MacLeod, ed. J. C. Watson (Glasgow, 1934).
G	*Geirfa Barddoniaeth Gynnar Gymraeg*, compiled J. Lloyd-Jones (Cardiff, 1931–52).
GCC	D. Simon Evans, *Gramadeg Cymraeg Canol* (Cardiff, 1951).
GPC	*Geiriadur Prifysgol Cymru* (University of Wales Dictionary) (Cardiff, 1950–).
	Gwaith Tudur Aled, ed. T. Gwynn Jones (Cardiff, 1926).
HW	J. E. Lloyd, *A History of Wales* (London, 1911).
HL	Sir John Rhŷs, *Hibbert Lectures* (London, 1888).
IEW	J. Strachan, *An Introduction to Early Welsh* (2nd ed., Manchester, 1937).
	K. H. Jackson, *Language and History in Early Britain* (Edinburgh, 1953).
Krappe	A. H. Krappe, 'Bendigeit Vran,' in *Études Celtiques* iii. 27–37.

BIBLIOGRAPHY

	Timothy Lewis, *Mabinogi Cymru* (Aberystwyth, 1931).
	Literary Tradition in the Old Norse and Celtic World (N. K. Chadwick, in *Saga Book*, vol. xiv, Part 11).
L & P	Henry Lewis and Holger Pedersen, *A Concise Comparative Celtic Grammar* (Göttingen, 1937)
Mac Cana	Proinsias Mac Cana, *Branwen Daughter of Llŷr* (Cardiff, 1958).
Math	W. J. Gruffydd, *Math vab Mathonwy* (Cardiff, 1928).
MU	*Mesca Ulad*, ed. J. C. Watson (Dublin, 1941).
	L. Mühlhausen, *Die vier Zweige des Mabinogi* (Halle, 1925).
	Cecile O'Rahilly, *Ireland and Wales* (London, 1924).
P	Peniarth MS. 6.
PKM	*Pedeir Keinc y Mabinogi*, ed. Ifor Williams (Cardiff, 1930).
	Syr T. H. Parry-Williams, *Pedair Cainc y Mabinogi wedi eu diweddaru* (Cardiff, 1937).
Pwyll	*Pwyll Pendeuic Dyuet*, ed. R. L. Thomson (Dublin, 1957).
R	*Red Book of Hergest*.
	William Rees, *An Historical Atlas of Wales* (Cardiff, 1951).
RC	*Revue Celtique* (Paris, 1870–1934).
Rhiannon	W. J. Gruffydd, *Rhiannon, An Inquiry into the First and Third Branches of the Mabinogi* (Cardiff, 1953).
SEBH	*Studies in Early British History*, ed. N. K. Chadwick (Cambridge, 1954).
SGS	*Scottish Gaelic Studies* (Oxford, 1926–).
	Togail Bruidne Da Derga, ed. E. Knott (Dublin, 1936).
	Les Mabinogion, trans. J. Loth (2nd ed., Paris, 1913).
	The Mabinogion..., trans. Lady Charlotte Guest (London, 1838–49).

	The Mabinogion, trans. T. P. Ellis and J. Lloyd (Oxford, 1929).
	The Mabinogion, trans. Gwyn Jones and Thomas Jones (Everyman ed., 1949).
	The Text of the Mabinogion and Other Welsh Tales from the Red Book of Hergest, ed. Sir John Rhŷs and J. Gwenogvryn Evans (Oxford 1887).
	The White Book Mabinogion, ed. J. Gwenogvryn Evans (Pwllheli, 1907).
W	*White Book of Rhydderch*.
WAL	R. S. Loomis, *Wales and the Arthurian Legend* (Cardiff, 1956).
	R. S. Loomis, *Arthurian Literature in the Middle Ages* (Oxford, 1959).
WG	Sir John Morris-Jones, *A Welsh Grammar* (Oxford, 1913).
WP	Sir John Rhŷs and D. Brynmor-Jones, *The Welsh People* (London, 1906).
WS	Sir John Morris-Jones, *Welsh Syntax* (Cardiff, 1931).
ZCP	*Zeitschrift für celtische Philologie* (Halle, 1897–).

ABBREVIATIONS

(Grammatical, &c.)

adj.	adjective, adjectival	mut.	mutation, mutated form
adv.	adverb		
aff.	affixed	n.	note
affirm.	affirmative	nas.	nasal, nasalising
art.	article	neg.	negative
asp.	aspirating, followed by spirant mutation	neut.	neuter
		num.	numeral
		O.E.	Old English
aux.	auxiliary	O.I.	Old Irish
coll.	collective	O.W.	Old Welsh
compar.	comparative	obj.	object, objective
conj.	conjunction	ord. num.	ordinal numeral
consuet.	consuetudinal	part.	particle
def. art.	definite article	perf.	perfect
demon.	demonstrative	pers.	personal
dep.	dependent	pl.	plural
eq.	equative	pluperf.	pluperfect
f.	feminine	poss.	possessive
fut.	future	prep.	preposition
Gael.	Gaelic (sometimes used to include Irish and Scottish Gaelic)	prep. pron.	prepositional pronoun
		pres.	present
		pret.	preterite
gen.	genitive	pron.	pronoun
I.W.	Ifor Williams	pronom.	pronominal
imperf.	imperfect	redup.	reduplicated
impers.	impersonal	refl.	reflexive
impv.	imperative	rel.	relative
ind.	indicative	Sc. G.	Scottish Gaelic
indep.	independent	sg.	singular
inf.	infixed	spir.	spirant
infin.	infinitive	subj.	subjunctive
intens.	intensive	subjt.	subject, subjective
interj.	interjection	subst.	substantive
interr.	interrogative	superl.	superlative
Ir.	Irish.	transl.	translate(d)
len.	lenition, leniting	v.	(textual) variant
lit.	literally	vn.	verbal noun
m.	masculine	vb.	verb
Med. W.	Medieval Welsh	:	cognate with
Mid. Ir.	Middle Irish	<	from
Mod. W.	Modern Welsh	>	developing into, giving

BRANWEN UERCH LYR

Bendigeiduran uab Llyr a oed urenhin coronawc ar yr ynys hon, ac ardyrchawc o goron Lundein. A frynhawngueith[1] yd oed yn Hardlech yn Ardudwy, yn llys idaw. Ac yn eisted yd oedynt ar garrec Hardlech, uch penn y weilgi, a Manawydan uab Llyr y urawt y gyt ac ef, a deu uroder un uam ac ef, Nissyen ac Efnyssyen, a guyrda y am hynny, mal y gwedei ynghylch brenhin. Y deu uroder un uam ac ef, meibon oedynt y Eurosswyd o'e uam ynteu Penardun, uerch Ueli uab Mynogan. A'r neill o'r gueisson hynny, gwas da oed: ef a barei [2]tangneued y rwg y deu lu, ban[2] uydynt lidyawcaf: sef oed hwnnw Nissyen. Y llall a barei ymlad [3]y rwng[3] y deu uroder, ban[4] uei uwyaf yd ymgerynt.

Ac ual yd oedynt yn eisted yuelly,[5] wynt a welynt teir llong ar dec, yn dyuot o deheu Iwerdon, ac yn kyrchu parth ac attunt, (39)* a cherdet rugyl ebrwyd ganthunt, y gwynt yn eu hol, ac [6]yn nessau[6] yn ebrwyd attunt. 'Mi a welaf longeu racco,' heb y brenhin, 'ac yn dyuot yn hy[7] parth a'r tir. Ac erchwch y wyr y llys wiscaw amdanunt,[8] a mynet y edrych pa uedwl yw yr eidunt.' Y gwyr a [9]wiscawd amdanunt[9] ac a nessayssant attunt y wayret. Gwedy guelet y llongeu o agos, diheu oed ganthunt na welsynt eiryoet[10] llongeu [11]gyweirach eu hansawd noc wy.[11] Arwydon tec, [12]guedus, arwreid o bali oed[12] arnunt.

Ac ar hynny, nachaf un o'r llongeu yn raculaenu rac y rei ereill, ac y guelynt dyrchauael taryan yn uch no bwrd y llong,

---

[1] phrynhawngweith. [2] dangneued y rwng y deulu, pan.
[3] rwng. [4] pan. [5] uelly. [6] yn eu nessau. [7] yn ebrwyd. [8] ymdanunt. [9] wiscwys ymdanunt. [10] *Omitted*.
[11] gyweiryach y hansawd noc wynt. [12] gwedus o bali a oed.

* The numbers within brackets refer to the columns of the White Book.

a swch y taryan[1] y uynyd yn arwyd tangneued. Ac y nessawys
y gwyr attunt, ual yd ymglywynt ymdidan. Bwrw badeu allan
a wnaethont[2] wynteu, a nessau parth a'r tir, a chyuarch guell
y'r brenhin. E[3] brenhin a'e clywei wynteu o'r lle yd oed ar
garrec uchel uch eu penn. 'Duw a rodo[4] da ywch,' heb ef, 'a
grayssaw wrthywch. Pieu [5]yniuer y llongeu[5] hynn, a phwy yssyd
pennaf[6] arnunt wy?' 'Arglwyd,' heb wynt, [7]'mae ymma[7]
Matholwch brenhin Iwerdon, ac ef bieu y llongeu.' 'Beth,' heb
y brenhin, 'a uynnhei ef? A uyn ef dyuot y'r tir?' 'Na uynn,
Arglwyd,' heb wynt, 'negessawl (40) yw wrthyt ti, onyt y neges
a geif.' 'By[8] ryw neges yw yr eidaw ef?' heb y brenhin. 'Mynnu
ymgyuathrachu a thidy, Arglwyd,' heb wynt. 'Y erchi Branwen
uerch Lyr y doeth,[9] ac os da genhyt ti, ef a uyn ymrwymaw
Ynys y Kedeirn ac Iwerdon y gyt, ual y bydynt gadarnach.'
'Ie,' heb ynteu, 'doet y'r tir, a chynghor a gymerwn ninheu am
hynny.' Yr atteb hwnnw a aeth ataw ef. 'Minheu a af yn llawen,'
heb ef. Ef a doeth y'r tir, a llawen uuwyt wrthaw; a dygyuor
mawr uu[10] yn y llys y nos honno, y rwng [11]e yniuer ef ac yniuer[11]
y llys.

Yn y lle trannoeth,[12] kymryt kynghor. Sef a gahat yn y
kynghor,[13] rodi Branwen y Uatholwch. A honno oed tryded[14]
prif rieni yn yr ynys hon; teccaf morwyn yn y byt oed.
A gwneuthur oed yn Aberfraw y gyscu genti,[15] ac odyno y
kychwyn.[16] Ac y kychwynassant [17]yr yniueroed[17] hynny parth
ac[18] Aberfraw, Matholwch [19]a'y yniueroed[19] yn y llongheu,
Bendigeituran [20]a'y niuer[20] ynteu ar tir, yny doethant hyt yn
Aberfraw.

Yn Aberfraw dechreu y wled, ac eisted. Sef ual yd eistedyssant: brenhin Ynys y Kedeirn a Manawydan uab Llyr o'r

---

[1] daryan.   [2] wnaethant.   [3] Y *et passim.*   [4] rodho.   [5] y niuer llongeu *sic leg.?*   [6] bennaf.   [7] y mae yma.   [8] py.   [9] ef *added.*   [10] a vu.   [11] y niueroed ef a niue- roed.   [12] drannoeth.   [13] hwnnw *added.*   [14] dryded.   [15] genthi.   [16] gychwynnu.   [17] y niueroed.   [18] ac ac.   [19] ae niueroed.   [20] ae niueroed.

BRANWEN UERCH LYR

¹neill parth idaw,¹ a Matholwch o'r parth arall, a Branwen uerch Lyr gyt ac ynteu.

Nyt ymywn ty yd oydynt, namyn ymywn palleu. ²Ny angassei² Uendigeituran eiryoet ymywn³ ty.

(41) A'r gyuedach a dechreussant. Dilit y gyuedach a wnaethant ac ymdidan. A phan welsant uot⁴ yn well udunt kymryt hun no dilyt kyuedach, y gyscu yd aethant. A'r nos honno y kyscwys Matholwch ⁵gan Uranwen.⁵ A thrannoeth, kyuodi a orugant pawb o niuer y llys; a'r swydwyr a dechreusant⁶ ymaruar am rannyat y meirych a'r gweisson. Ac eu rannu a wnaethant ym pob kyueir hyt y mor. Ac ar hynny dydgueith, nachaf Efnyssen ⟨y⟩ gwr anagneuedus⁷ a dywedassam⁸ uchot, yn dywanu y lety meirch Matholwch, a gouyn a wnaeth, pioed y meirch. 'Meirych Matholwch brenhin Iwerdon yw y rei hyn,' heb wy. 'Beth a wnant wy yna?'⁹ heb ef. 'Yma y mae brenhin Iwerdon, ac yr gyscwys gan Uranwen dy chwaer,¹⁰ a'y ueirych yw y rei hynn.' ¹¹'Ay yuelly¹¹ y gwnaethant wy am uorwyn kystal a honno, ac yn chwaer y minheu, y rodi heb uyghanyat¹² i? Ny ellynt wy tremic uwy arnaf i,'¹³ heb ef. Ac yn hynny guan¹⁴ y dan y meirych, a thorri y guefleu wrth y danned udunt, a'r clusteu wrth y penneu, a'r rawn wrth y keuyn; ¹⁵ac ny caei graf ar yr amranneu, eu llad wrth¹⁵ yr ascwrn. A gwneuthur anfuryf ar y meirych yuelly,¹⁶ hyd nat oed rym a ellit a'r meirych.

E¹⁷ chwedyl a doeth at Uatholwch. Sef ual y doeth: dywedut (42) anfuruaw y ueirych ac eu llygru, hyt nat oed un mwynyant¹⁸ a ellit ohonunt. 'Ie, Arglwyd,' ¹⁹heb un,¹⁹ 'dy waradwydaw yr²⁰ a wnaethpwyt, a hynny a uynhir y wneuthur ²¹a thi.'²¹ 'Dioer,

---

¹ neillparth. ² nyt eyngassei. ³ mywn. ⁴ bot.
⁵ a Brannwen y gyt. ⁶ dechreuassant. ⁷ an hagneuedus.
⁸ ni *added*. ⁹ yma. ¹⁰ whaer. ¹¹ ae uelly.
¹² vygkennyat. ¹³ no hwnnw *added*. ¹⁴ gwan. ¹⁵ ar ny chaei graf ar yr amranneu y lladei wrth. ¹⁶ uelly. ¹⁷ Y
¹⁸ mwynant. ¹⁹ heb yr vn. ²⁰ *Omitted*. ²¹ ytti.

¹eres genhyf,¹ os uy gwaradwydaw a uynhynt, rodi morwyn gystal, kyuurd, gyn² anwylet gan y chenedyl, ac a rodyssant ym.' 'Arglwyd,' heb un arall, 'ti a wely ³dangos ef.³ Ac nyt oes it a wnelych namyn kyrchu dy longeu.' Ac ar hynny arouun y longeu a wnaeth ef.

E chwedyl a doeth at Uendigeituran bot Matholwch yn adaw y llys, ⁴heb ouyn, heb ganhyat.⁴ A chenadeu a aeth y ouyn idaw paham oed hynny. Sef kennadeu a aeth, Idic uab Anarawc ac Eueyd Hir. Y guyr hynny ⁵a'y godiwawd,⁵ ac a ouynyssant idaw, pa darpar oed yr eidaw, a pha achaws yd oed yn mynet ⁶e ymdeith.⁶ 'Dioer,' heb ynteu, 'pei ys gwypwn, ny down yma. Cwbyl waradwyd a geueis. Ac ny duc neb kyrch waeth ⁷no'r dugum ymma.⁷ A reuedawt rygyueryw⁸ a mi.' 'Beth yw hynny?' heb wynt. 'Rodi Bronwen⁹ uerch Lyr ym, yn tryded prif rieni yr ynys honn, ac yn uerch y urenhin Ynys y Kedeyrn, a chyscu genthi, a gwedy hynny uy gwaradwydaw. A ryued oed genhyf, nat kyn rodi morwyn gystal a honno ym y gwneit y (43) gwaradwyd a wnelit ym.' 'Dioer, Arglwyd, nyt o uod y neb a uedei y llys,' heb wynt, 'na neb o'e kynghor¹⁰ y gwnaet⟨h⟩pwyt y gwaradwyd hwnnw yt.¹¹ A chyt bo gwaradwyd gennyt ti hynny, mwy yw gan Uendigeituran no chenyt ti, y tremic hwnnw a'r guare.' 'Ie,' heb ef, 'mi a tebygaf. Ac eissoes ni eill ef uy niwaradwydaw i o hynny.'

E gwyr hynny a ymchwelwys¹² a'r atteb hwnnw, parth a'r lle yd oed Uendigeituran, a menegi idaw yr atteb a diwedyssei¹³ Uatholwch. 'Ie,' heb ynteu, 'nyt oes ymwaret e¹⁴ uynet ef yn anygneuedus, ac nys gadwn.' 'Ie, Arglwyd,' heb wy, 'anuon etwa genhadeu yn y ol.' 'Anuonaf,' heb ef. 'Kyuodwch, Uanawydan uab Llyr, ac Eueyd Hir, ac Unic Glew Yscwyd, ac ewch yn y ol,' heb ef, 'a menegwch idaw, ef a geif march

---

¹ eres yw gennyf.   ² kyn.   ³ dangos mae ef.   ⁴ heb ovyn kenyat.   ⁵ ae gordiwedawd   ⁶ ymeith.   ⁷ noc a dugum i yma.   ⁸ rygynneryw.   ⁹ Brannwen.
¹⁰ gyghor.   ¹¹ ytti.   ¹² ymchoelassant.   ¹³ rodassei.
¹⁴ oe *sic leg.*?

iach am pob¹ un o'r a lygrwyt; ac y gyt a hynny, ef a geif yn
wynepwerth² idaw llathen³ aryant a uo kyuref ⟨a'e uys bychan⁴⟩
a chyhyt ac ef e hun, a chlawr eur kyflet a'y wyneb; a menegwch
ydaw pa⁵ ryw wr a wnaeth hynny, a phan yw o'm anuod inheu 115
y gwnaethpwyt hynny; ac y may brawt un uam a mi a wnaeth
hynny, ac nat hawd genhyf i⁶ na'e lad⁷ na'e diuetha; a doet y
ymwelet a mi,' hef ef, 'a mi a wnaf y dangneued ar y llun (44) y
mynho⁸ e hun.'

E kennadeu a aethant ar ol Matholwch, ac a uanagyssant 120
idaw yr ymadrawd hwnnw yn garedic, ac ef a'e guerendewis.⁹
'A wyr,' heb ef, 'ni a gymerwn gynghor.' Ef a aeth yn y gynghor.
Sef kynghor a uedylyssant:¹⁰ os gwrthot hynny a wnelynt, bot
yn tebygach¹¹ ganthunt cael kywilid a uei uwy no chael iawn
a uei uwy.¹² A disgynnu a wnaeth ar gymryt hynny. Ac y'r llys 125
y deuthant¹³ yn dangneuedus. A chyweiraw¹⁴ y pebylleu a'r
palleu a wnaethant udunt ar ureint kyweirdeb yneuad,¹⁵ a
mynet y uwyta. Ac ual y dechreuyssant eisted ar dechreu y
wled, yd eistedyssant yna.

A dechreu ymdidan a wnaeth Matholwch a Bendigeituran. 130
Ac nachaf yn ardiawc gan Uendigeituran y⟨r⟩¹⁶ ymdidan, ac yn
drist,¹⁷ a gaei gan Uatholwch, a'y lywenyt yn wastat kyn no
hynny. A medylyaw a wnaeth¹⁸ bot yn athrist gan yr unben
uychanet a gawssei o iawn am y gam. 'A wr,' heb y Bendigeiduran, 'nit wyt gystal ymdidanwr heno ac un nos. Ac os yr 135
bychanet¹⁹ genhyt ti dy iawn, ti a gehy²⁰ ychwanegu yt wrth dy
uynnu,²¹ ac auory talu dy ueirch yt.' 'Arglwyd,' heb ef, 'Duw a
dalo yt.' 'Mi a deledwaf dy iawn heuyt yt,' heb y Bendigeituran.
'Mi a rodaf yt peir, a chynnedyf y peir yw, (45) y gwr a lader

---

¹ bop. ² wynabwarth. ³ llatheu. ⁴ *Supplied by Sir Ifor Williams in* PKM. ⁵ py. ⁶ ynheu. ⁷ ef *added*. ⁸ mynno. ⁹ gwarandewis. ¹⁰ uedylyassant. ¹¹ debygach. ¹² gymeint (*this is entered above the line in* R). ¹³ doethant. ¹⁴ chweiryaw. ¹⁵ neuad. ¹⁶ yn *in both* W *and* R. ¹⁷ am y warth *added*. ¹⁸ oruc. ¹⁹ bychenet. ²⁰ gey. ²¹ dy hun *added*.

hediw yt, y uwrw yn y peir, ac erbyn auory y uot yn gystal ac y bu oreu, eithyr na byd llyueryd ganthaw.' A diolwch a wnaeth ynteu hynny, a diruawr lywenyd a gymerth ynteu[1] o'r achaws hwnnw. A thrannoeth y talwyt y ueirych idaw, tra barhawd[2] meirych dof. Ac odyna y kyrchwyt ac ef kymwt arall, ac y talwyt ebolyon ydaw, yny uu gwbyl idaw y dal. Ac wrth hynny y dodet ar y kymwt hwnnw, o hynny allan, Tal Ebolyon.

A'r eil nos, eisted y gyt a wnaethant. 'Arglwyd,' heb y Matholwch, 'pan doeth yti y peir a rodeist ymi?' 'E[3] doeth im,' heb ef, 'y gan wr a uu y'th wlat ti. Ac ni wn na bo yno y caffo.' 'Pwy oed hwnnw?' heb ef. 'Llassar Llaes Gyfnewit,' heb ef. 'A hwnnw a doeth yma o Iwerdon, a Chymidei Kymeinuoll, y wreic, y gyt ac ef, ac a dianghyssant o'r ty hayarn yn Iwerdon pan wnaethpwyt yn wenn[4] yn eu kylch, ac y dianghyssant[5] odyno. Ac eres[6] gynhyf i ony wdosti[7] dim y wrth hynny.'

'Gwn, Arglwyd,' heb ef, 'a chymeint ac a wnn, mi a'e managaf yti. Yn hela yd oedwn yn Iwerdon dydgueith ar benn go⟨r⟩ssed[8] [9]uch penn llyn oed[9] yn Iwerdon, a Llyn y Peir y gelwit. A mi a welwn gwr melyngoch mawr, yn dyuot o'r llyn, a pheir ar y geuyn. A gwr heuyt[10] athrugar mawr, a drygweith[11] anorles[12] arnaw oed; a gwreic yn y ol; ac ot (46) oed uawr ef, mwy dwyweith oed y wreic noc ef. A chyrchu ataf a wnaethant, a [13]chyuarch uell[13] im.' 'Ie,' heb ymi, 'pa gerdet yssyd arnawch chwi?' [14]'Llyna gerdet yssyd arnam ni, Arglwyd,'[14] heb ef: 'y wreic honn,' [15]heb ef,[15] 'ym penn pethewnos a mis, y byd beichogi idi, a'r mab a aner yna o'r torllwyth hwnnw, ar benn y pethewnos a'r mi,[16] y byd gwr ymlad llawn aruawc.'

'Y kymereis inheu [17]wyntwy arnaf, yu gossymdeithaw:[17] y[18]

---

[1] yndaw. [2] barhaawd. [3] Ef a. [4] wynnyas *sic leg.*?
[5] dihangyssant. [6] yw *added*. [7] wdost ti. [8] W *has* gossed, R gorsed. [9] a oed uch pen llynn. [10] *Omitted*. [11] drycweith.
[12] auorles. [13] chyfuarch gwell. [14] Llyna y ryw gerdet Arglwyd yssyd arnam ni. [15] *Omitted*.
[16] W *has* mi, R mis *sic leg*. [17] arnaf y gossymdeithaw wyntwy.
[18] ac y.

buant ulwydyn¹ gyt a mi. Yn y ulwydyn y keueis yn diwarauun
wynt; o hynny allann y guarauunwyt im. A chyn penn y pedwyryd ⟨mis²⟩ wynt eu hun yn peri eu hatcassu,³ ac anghynwys
yn y wlat, yn gwneuthur sarahedeu,⁴ ac yn eighaw ac yn
gouudyaw guyrda a gwragedda. O hynny allan y dygyuores
uyg kyuoeth am ym⁵ pen y erchi im ymuadeu ac wynt, a rodi
dewis im, ae uyg kyuoeth ae wynt.

'E dodeis inheu ar gynghor uy gwlat beth a wneit⁶ amdanunt.
Nyd eynt wy o'y bod; nit oed reit udunt wynteu ⁷oc eu⁷
hanuod, herwyd ymlad, uynet. Ac yna yn y kyuyng gynghor,
y causant gwneuthur ystauell haearn oll; a gwedy bot y barawt
yr ystauell, dyuyn⁸ a oed o of yn Iwerdon yno, o'r a oed o
⁹perchen geuel a mwrthwl,⁹ a pheri gossot kyuuch a chrib yr
ystauell o lo, a pheri guassanaethu (47) yn diwall o uwyt a llyn
arnunt, ar y wreic, a'y gwr, a'y phlant. A phan wybuwyt eu
medwi wynteu, y dechreuwyt¹⁰ kymyscu y tan a'r glo am ben yr
ystauell, a chwythu y megineu ¹¹a oed wedy eu gossot yg kylch
y ty, a gwr a pob dwy uegin, a dechreu chwythu y megineu¹¹
yny uyd y ty yn burwen am eu penn. Ac yna y bu y kynghor
ganthunt hwy¹² ymherued¹³ llawr yr ystauell; ac yd arhoes ef yny
uyd y pleit haearn yn wenn. Ac rac diruawr wres, y kyrchwys y
bleit¹⁴ a'e yscwyd a'y tharaw gantaw allan, ac yn y ol ynteu y
wreic. A neb ni dieghis¹⁵ odyna¹⁶ namyn ef a'e wreic. Ac yna
o'm tebygu i, Arglwyd,' heb y Matholwch wrth Uendigeiduran,
'y doeth ef drwod attat ti.' 'Yna dioer,' heb ynteu, 'y doeth
yma, ac y roes¹⁷ y peir y minheu.' 'Pa delw, Arglwyd, yd erbyn-
neisti¹⁸ wynteu?' 'Eu rannu ym pob lle yn y kyuoeth, ac y maent
yn lluossauc, ac yn dyrchauael ym pob lle, ac yn cadarnhau y¹⁹
uann y bythont,²⁰ o wyr ac arueu goreu a welas neb.'

---

¹ y *added.* ² *Omitted in* W. ³ hatgassau. ⁴ sarhaedeu.
⁵ vym. ⁶ wnelit. ⁷ oe. ⁸ dyuynnu.
⁹ berchen geueyl a myrthwl. ¹⁰ dechreuit. ¹¹ *Omitted.*
¹² *Omitted.* ¹³ ym perued. ¹⁴ pleit. ¹⁵ dihengis.
¹⁶ odyno. ¹⁷ rodes. ¹⁸ erbynneist ti. ¹⁹ yn y.
²⁰ bont.

BRANWEN UERCH LYR

Dilit ymdidan a wnaethant y nos honno, tra uu da ganthunt, a cherd a chyuedach. A phan welsant uot yn llessach udunt uynet y gyscu noc eisted a wei¹ hwy, y gyscu yd aethant. Ac
200 yuelly y treulyssant y wled honno drwy² digriuwch. Ac (48) yn niwed hynny, y kychwynnwys Matholwch, a Branuen y³ gyt ac ef, parth ac Iwerdon. A hynny o Abermenei y kychwynnyssant teir llong ar dec, ac y doethant hyt yn Iwerdon.

Yn Iwerdon, dirwawr⁴ lywenyd a uu wrthunt. Ny doey wr
205 mawr, na gwreic da yn Iwerdon, e ymw⟨e⟩let⁵ a Branwen, ni rodei hi ae cae ae modrwy ae teyrndlws cadwedic ydaw, a uei arbennic y welet yn mynet ⁶e ymdeith.⁶ Ac ymysc hynny, y ulwydyn honno a duc hi yn glotuawr, a hwyl delediw a duc hi o glot a chedymdeithon. ⁷Ac yn hynny, beichogi a damweinwys
210 idi y gael.⁷ A guedy treulaw yr amseroyd dylyedus, mab a anet idi. Sef enw a dodet ⁸ar y mab,⁸ Guern uab Matholwch. Rodi y mab ar uaeth a wnaethpwyt ar⁹ un lle goreu y wyr yn Iwerdon.

A hynny yn yr eil ulwydyn, llyma ymodwrd yn Iwerdon am y guaradwyd a gawssei Matholwch¹⁰ yg Kymry, a'r somm a
215 wnathoedit idaw am y ueirch. A hynny y urodyr maeth, a'r gwyr¹¹ nessaf gantaw, yn lliwaw idaw hynny, a¹² heb y gelu. A¹³ nachaf y dygyuor yn Iwerdon hyt nat oed lonyd idaw ony chaei dial y sarahet.¹⁴ Sef dial a wnaethant, gyrru Branwen o un ystauell ac ef, a'y chymell y bobi yn y llys, a pheri y'r kygyd,
220 gwedy¹⁵ bei yn dryllyaw kic, dyuot idi a tharaw bonclust arnei beunyd. Ac yuelly¹⁶ (49) y gwnaethpwyt y foen.¹⁷ 'Ie, Arglwyd,' heb y wyr wrth Uatholwch, 'par weithon wahard y llongeu, a'r yscraffeu,¹⁸ a'r corygeu, ual nat el neb y Gymry; ac a del yma o Gymry, carchara wynt ¹⁹⟨ac⟩ na at trachefyn,¹⁹ rac gwybot
225 hynn.' Ac ar hynny y diskynyssant.

---

¹ uei.   ² trwy.   ³ *Omitted*.   ⁴ diruawr.   ⁵ ymwelet.
⁶ ymeith.   ⁷ A beichogi a damweinwys idi y gael yn hynny.
⁸ arnaw.   ⁹ R yr. *Read* y'r.   ¹⁰ Vatholwch.   ¹¹ rei.
¹² *Omitted*.   ¹³ ac.   ¹⁴ sarhaet.   ¹⁵ y *added*.   ¹⁶ uelly.
¹⁷ phoen.   ¹⁸ ysgraffeu.   ¹⁹ R hyt nat elont dracheuyn, W na na at .... *See note*.

Blwynyded nit llei no their y buant yuelly.¹ Ac yn hynny,
meithryn ederyn drydwen a wnaeth hitheu ar dal y noe gyt
a hi, a dyscu ieith idi, a menegi y'r ederyn y ryw wr oed y brawt.
A dwyn llythyr y poeneu a'r amharch a oed arnei hitheu. A'r
llythyr a rwymwyt am uon eskyll yr ederyn, a'y anuon parth 230
a Chymry, a'r ederyn a doeth y'r ynys honn. Sef lle y cauas
Uendigeiduran, yg Kaer Seint yn Aruon, yn dadleu idaw
dydgweith. A diskynnu ar e yscwyd, a garwhau y phluf, yny
arganuuwyt y llythyr, ac adnabot meithryn yr ederyn yg
kyuanned. Ac yna kymryt y llythyr a'y edrych. A phan 235
darllewyt y llythyr, doluryaw a wnaeth² o glybot y poen³ oed
ar Uranwen, a dechreu o'r lle hwnnw peri⁴ anuon kennadeu y
dygyuoryaw yr ynys honn y gyt. Ac yna y peris ef dyuot llwyr
wys ⁵pedeir degwlat⁵ a seithugeint hyt attaw, ac e hun cwynaw
wrth hynny, bot y poen a oed ar y chwaer. Ac yna kymryt 240
kynghor. Sef kynghor a gahat, kyrchu Iwerdon, ac adaw
seithwyr ⁶y dywyssogyon⁶ yma, a Chradawc uab Bran y⁷ benhaf, ac eu seith (50) marchawc. Yn Edeirnon yd edewit y gwyr
hynny, ac o achaws hynny y dodet Seith Marchawc ar y dref.
Sef seithwyr oedynt, Cradawc uab Bran, ac Euehyd⁸ Hir, ac 245
Unic Glew Yscwyd, ac Idic uab Anarawc Walltgrwn, a Fodor
uab Eruyll, ac Wlch Minasgwrn,⁹ a Llashar uab Llayssar¹⁰
Llaesgygwyt, a Phendaran Dyuet¹¹ yn was ieuanc gyt ac wy.
Y seith hynny a drigwys¹² yn seith kynueissat y synyaw ar yr
ynys honn, a Chradawc uab Bran yn benhaf kynweisyat 250
arnunt.

Bendigeiduran, a'r yniuer¹³ a dywedyssam ni, a hwylyssant¹⁴
parth ac Iwerdon, ac nyt oed uawr y weilgi yna: y ueis yd aeth
ef. Nyt oed namyn dwy auon: Lli ac Archan y gelwit. A guedy
hynny yd amlawys¹⁵ y weilgi, ¹⁶pan oreskynwys y weilgi¹⁶ y 255

¹ uelly. ² Bendigeituran *added*. ³ a *added*. ⁴ *Omitted*.
⁵ pedeir gwlat. ⁶ yn tywyssogyon. ⁷ yn. ⁸ Eueyd.
⁹ Minascwrn. ¹⁰ Llaesar. ¹¹ W *repeats* Dyuet.
¹² dricywys. ¹³ niuer. ¹⁴ hwylyassant ¹⁵ amylhawys.
¹⁶ *Omitted*.

tyrnassoed. Ac yna y kerdwys ef ac a oed ¹o gerd¹ arwest ar
y geuyn e hun, a chyrchu tir Iwerdon.

A meicheit Matholwch ²a oedynt² ar lan y weilgi ³dydgueith,
yn troi yg kylch eu moch. Ac o achaws e dremynt a welsant ar
260 y weilgi,³ wy⁴ a doethant at Matholwch.⁵ 'Arglwyd,' heb vy,
'henpych guell.' 'Duw a rodo da ywch,' heb ef, 'a chwedleu
genhwch.'⁶ 'Arglwyd,' heb wy, 'mae genhym ni chwedleu
ryued:⁷ coet rywelsom ar y weilgi, yn y lle ny welsam eiryoet
un prenn.' 'Llyna beth eres,' heb ef. 'A welewch wchi⁸ dim
265 namyn hynny?' 'Gwelem, Arglwyd,' heb wy, 'mynyd (51) mawr
gyr⁹ llaw y coet, a hwnnw ar gerdet; ac eskeir aruchel ar y
mynyd, a llynn o pop parth y'r¹⁰ eskeir; a'r coet, a'r mynyd, a
phob peth ¹¹oll o hynny¹¹ ar gerdet.' 'Ie,' heb ynteu, 'nyt oes
neb yma a wypo dim y wrth hynny, onys gwyr Branwen.
270 Gouynnwch idi.' Kennadeu a aeth at Uranwen. 'Arglwydes,'
heb wy, 'beth dybygy di yw hynny?' ¹²'Kyn ny bwyf arglwydes,'
heb hi, 'mi a wnn beth yw hynny:¹² gwyr Ynys y Kedyrn yn
dyuot drwod¹³ o glybot uym poen¹⁴ a'm amharch.'¹⁵ 'Beth yw
y coet a welat ar y mor?' heb wy. ¹⁶'Gwernenni llongeu¹⁶ a
275 hwylbrenni,' heb hi. 'Och,' heb wy, 'beth oed y mynyd a welit
gan ystlys y llongeu?' 'Bendigeiduran ¹⁷uym brawt,'¹⁷ heb hi,
'oed hwnnw, yn dyuot y ueis. Nyd oed long y kynghanei ef
yndi.' 'Beth oed yr eskeir aruchel a'r llynn o bop parth y'r
eskeir?' 'Ef,' heb hi, 'yn edrych ar yr ynys honn, llidyawc yw.
280 Y deu lygat ef o pop parth y drwyn yw y dwy lynn o bop parth
y'r eskeir.'

Ac yna dygyuor holl wyr ymlad Iwerdon a wnaethpwyt y
gyt, a'r holl uorbennyd¹⁸ yn gyflym, a chynghor a gymerwyt.

---

¹ *added suprascript in* W. R *gives this reading.* ² oed.
³ *Omitted.*   ⁴ wynt.   ⁵ Vatholwch   ⁶ y gennwch
sic leg.?   ⁷ enryued.   ⁸ R chwi *sic leg.*   ⁹ geir.
¹⁰ or.   ¹¹ o hynny ol.   ¹² *Omitted.*   ¹³ drwad.
¹⁴ i *added.*   ¹⁵ hamarch.   ¹⁶ gwerneneu llogeu.   ¹⁷ vy
mrawt i.   ¹⁸ awnaethpwyt *followed here, but the scribe has
cancelled it.*

BRANWEN UERCH LYR

'Arglwyd,' heb y wyrda wrth Uatholwch, 'nyt oes gynghor namyn kilyaw drwy Linon (auon[1] oed yn Iwerdon),* a gadu Llinon y rot ac ef, a thorri y bont yssyd ar yr auon. (52) A mein sugyn yssyd ygwaelawt yr auon, ny eill na llong na llestyr arnei.' Wynt a gylyssant drwy yr auon, ac a torryssant y bont.[2]

Bendigeiduran a doeth y'r tir, a llynghes y gyt ac ef, parth a glann yr auon. 'Arglwyd,' heb y wyrda, 'ti a wdost kynnedyf yr auon, ny eill neb uynet drwydi, nyt oes bont arnei hitheu. Mae dy gynghor am bont?' heb wy. 'Nit oes,' heb ynteu, 'namyn a uo penn bit pont.[3] Mi[4] a uydaf pont',[5] heb ef. Ac yna gyntaf y dywetpwyt y geir hwnnw, ac y diharebir[6] etwa ohonaw.

Ac yna guedy gorwed ohonaw ef ar traws[7] yr auon, y byrwyt[8] clwydeu arnaw ef, ac yd aeth y luoed[9] ef [10]ar y draws ef drwod.[10] [11]Ar hynny,[11] gyt ac y kyuodes[12] ef, llyma gennadeu Matholwch[13] yn dyuot attaw ef,[14] ac yn kyuarch guell idaw, ac yn y annerch y gan Uatholwch y gyuathrachwr, ac yn menegi o'e uod ef na haedei[15] [16]arnaw ef namyn da.[16] 'Ac y mae Matholwch[17] yn rodi brenhinaeth Iwerdon y Wern uab Matholwch, dy nei ditheu, uab dy chwaer, ac yn y ystynnu[18] y'th wyd di, yn lle y cam a'r codyant a wnaethpwyt y Uranwen. Ac yn y lle y mynnych ditheu,[19] ay yma ay yn Ynys y Kedyrn, gossymdeitha Uatholwch.' 'Ie,' heb ynteu Uendigeiduran, 'ony allaf i ue hun cael y urenhinaeth, [20]ac aduyd[20] ys kymeraf[21] gynghor (53) am ych[22] kennadwri chwi. O hyn hyt [23]ban del amgen, ny cheffwch

---

[1] a *added*.   [2] pont.   [3] R *and* P bont.   [4] miui.
[5] R *and* P bont.   [6] R diaerebir, P diarhebir.   [7] P draws.
[8] R byrywyt, P byrywd.   [9] P lu.   [10] R ef *omitted*, P drwod ar y draws ef.   [11] P ac ar henny.   [12] kuodes.   [13] P Mallolwch *et passim*.   [14] *Omitted*.   [15] P haethei.
[16] R ef *omitted*, P namyn da arnaw ef.   [17] P hep wy *added*.
[18] R *and* P estynnu, P *adds* idaw.   [19] P arglwyt *added*.
[20] R ac atuyd, P oc oduyt.   [21] P kymerafy.   [22] P awch.

* The brackets are used here editorially to indicate that the phrase is in parenthesis.

y genhyf i attep.'²³ 'Ie,'¹ heb wynteu,² 'yr atteb goreu a gaffom ninheu, attat ti y³ down ac ef, ac aro ditheu yn kennadwri ninheu.' 'Arhoaf,'⁴ heb ef, 'o⁵ dowch yn ehegyr.'⁶

Y kennadeu a gyrchyssant⁷ racdu,⁸ ac at⁹ Uatholwch y doethant. 'Arglwyd,' heb wy, 'kyweira attep a uo gwell at¹⁰ Uendigeidwran. Ny warandawei dim o'r attep a aeth y¹¹ genhym ni attaw ef.'¹² 'A¹³ wyr,' heb y Matholwch, 'mae ¹⁴ych kynghor chwi?'¹⁴ ¹⁵'Arglwyd', heb wy, 'nyt oes it gynghor¹⁵ namyn un. Ni enghis¹⁶ ef ymywn ty eiryoet,' heb wy. ¹⁷'Gwna ty,' heb wy, 'o'y anryded ef, y ganho ef¹⁷ a gwyr Ynys y Kedyrn yn¹⁸ y neill parth¹⁹ ²⁰y'r ty,²⁰ a thitheu a'th lu ²¹yn y²¹ parth arall. A doro²² dy urenhinaeth yn y ewyllus, a gwra²³ idaw. Ac o enryded²⁴ gwneuthur y ty,' heb wy, 'peth ²⁵ny chauas²⁵ eiryoet²⁶ ty y ganhei²⁷ yndaw, ef a tangnoueda²⁸ a thi.' A'r kennadeu a doethant²⁹ a'r³⁰ gennadwri honno gantunt³¹ at³² Uendigeiduran; ac ynteu a gymerth gynghor.³³ Sef a gauas yn y gynghor, kymryt hynny; a thrwy gynghor Branuen uu hynny oll, ac rac llygru y wlat oed genti hitheu hynny.

³⁴E tangneued³⁴ a gyweirwyt,³⁵ a'r ty a adeilwyt yn uawr ac yn braf. Ac ystryw³⁶ a wnaeth y Gwydyl. Sef ystryw³⁷ a wnaethant, dodi guanas o bop parth (54) y bop colouyn o cant colouyn³⁸ oed yn y ty, a dodi boly croyn ar bop guanas,³⁹ a gwr aruawc

---

²³ R pan —, P hynny ny chewch chwi y gennyfi ateb eny del gennwch amgen noc a doeth. ¹ P arglwyt *added*. ² P wy.
³ R ni a. ⁴ P aroaf. ⁵ R a. ⁶ R ebrwyd.
⁷ R gychassant, P gerdassant. ⁸ P racdunt. ⁹ P ar.
¹⁰ P ar. ¹¹ *Omitted in* P. ¹² *Omitted in* R. ¹³ R Ha.
¹⁴ P y kygor. ¹⁵ P nyd oes id gygor arglwyt hep wy. ¹⁶ R eigwys, P ennis. ¹⁷ R gwna ty heb wynt y geingho ef, P gwna di hep wy oe anrydet ef ty y ganno ef. ¹⁸ P ar. ¹⁹ P stlys. ²⁰ P itaw. ²¹ P or. ²² R *and* P dyro.
²³ R gwrha, P gwrhaa. ²⁴ P anrydet. ²⁵ R nys kauas, P ny gafas. ²⁶ P eiroed. ²⁷ R geinghei. ²⁸ R tangneuedha, P dagnefeta. ²⁹ R aethant. ³⁰ P y *added*.
³¹ P *Omitted*. ³² P ar. ³³ P kymyrth. ³⁴ R y dangneued honno, P y dagnefet. ³⁵ P gyweirwd. ³⁶ P stryw.
³⁷ P stryw. ³⁸ R *adds* a. ³⁹ P un or gwnasseu.

¹ym pob vn ohonunt.¹ Sef a wnaeth Efnyssyen dyuot ymlaen²
llu Ynys y Kedyrn ymywn, ac edrych golygon orwyllt³
antrugarawc ar hyt y ty.⁴ Ac arganuot y bolyeu⁵ crwyn a
wnaeth ar hyt y pyst. 'Beth yssyd yn y boly hwnn?' heb ef,
wrth un o'r Gwydyl. 'Blawt, eneit,' heb ef. Sef a wnaeth ynteu, 335
y deimlaw⁶ ⁷hyt ban⁷ gauas y benn, a guascu y benn, yny
glyw y uyssed yn ymanodi yn y ureichell⁸ drwy yr ascwrn.
Ac adaw hwnnw, a dodi y law⁹ ar un arall a gouyn, 'Beth yssyd
yma?' 'Blawt,' medei y Gwydel. Sef a wnai¹⁰ ynteu yr un guare
a fawb¹¹ ohonunt,¹² hyt nat edewis ef wr¹³ byw o'r hollwyr o'r 340
deu cannwr eithyr un. A dyuot at¹⁴ hwnnw, a gouyn, 'Beth
yssyd yma?' 'Blawt, eneit,' heb y Gwydel. Sef a wnaeth ynteu,
y deimlaw ef yny gauas y benn, ac ual y guascassei benneu y
rei ereill, guascu penn hwnnw. Sef y clywei arueu am benn
hwnnw. Nyt ymedewis ef a hwnnw, yny ladawd.¹⁵ Ac yna canu 345
englyn:—

> Yssit yn y boly hwnn amryw ulawt,
> Keimeit, kynniuyeit, diskynneit yn trin,
> Rac kydwyr cadbarawt.

Ac ar hynny y dothyw y niueroed y'r ty. Ac y doeth gwyr¹⁶ Ynys 350
Iwer-(55)don y'r ty o'r neill parth, a gwyr¹⁷ Ynys y Kedyrn o'r
parth arall. Ac yn gyn ebrwydet ac yd eistedyssant y bu duundeb
y rydunt,¹⁸ ac yd ystynnwyt y urenhinaeth y'r mab.

Ac yna, guedy daruot y tangneued,¹⁹ galw o Uendigeiduran
y mab attaw. Y gan Uendigeiduran y kyrchawd y mab at 355
Uanawydan,²⁰ a phawb o'r a'e guelei yn y garu. E gan Uanawydan y gelwis Nyssyen uab Eurosswyd y mab attaw. Y mab

---

¹ P em hob un onadunt. ² R ym blaen. ³ P arwyllt.
⁴ P *adds* a wnaeth. ⁵ P byly. ⁶ P *adds* ef.
⁷ R hyt pan, P eny. ⁸ R vreithell, P ureithell *sic leg*.
⁹ P llaw. ¹⁰ R wnaey, P wnaei. ¹¹ R *and* P phawb.
¹² P o nadunt. ¹³ P gwr. ¹⁴ P ar. ¹⁵ R
lladawd. ¹⁶ o *added*. ¹⁷ o *added*. ¹⁸ ryngtunt.
¹⁹ dangued. ²⁰ Uanywydan.

a aeth attaw yn diryon. 'Paham,' heb yr Efnissyen, 'na daw uy nei, uab uy chwaer, attaf i? Kyn ny bei urenhin ar Iwerdon, da oed genhyf i ymtiryoni a'r mab.' 'Aet yn llawen,' heb y Bendigeiduran. Y mab a aeth attaw yn llawen. 'Y Duw y dygaf uyg kyffes,' heb ynteu yn y uedwl, 'ys anhebic a gyflauan gan y tylwyth y wneuthur,[1] a wnaf i yr awr honn.' A chyuodi y uynyd, a chymryt y mab [2]erwyd y traet,[2] [3]a heb ohir, na chael[3] o dyn yn y ty gauael arnaw, yny want y mab yn wysc y benn yn y gynneu.[4] A fan[5] welas Uranwen[6] y mab yn boeth yn y tan, hi a gynsynwys[7] uwrw neit yn y tan, o'r lle yd oed yn eisted rwng y deu uroder. A chael o Uendigeiduran hi yn y neill law, a'y tarean yn y llaw arall. Ac yna, ymgyuot[8] (56) o bawb ar hyt y ty. A llyna y godwrw mwyhaf a uu gan yniuer[9] un ty, pawb yn kymryt y arueu. Ac yna y dywot Mordwyd Tyllyon, 'Guern gwn, gwchuiwch Uordwyt Tyllyon.' Ac [10]yn yd[10] aeth pawb ym pen yr[11] arueu, y kynhelis Bendigeiduran Uranwen y rwng y taryan[12] a'y yscwyd.

Ac yna y dechrewis y Gwydyl kynneu tan dan y peir dadeni. Ac yna y byrywyt y kalaned yn y peir, yny uei yn llawn, ac y kyuodyn [13]tranoeth y bore[13] yn wyr ymlad kystal[14] a chynt, eithyr na ellynt dywedut. Ac yna pan welas Efnissyen y calaned heb enni yn un lle o wyr Ynys y Kedyrn, y dywot yn y uedwl, 'Oy a Duw,' heb ef, 'guae ui uy mot yn achaws y'r wydwic honn o wyr Ynys y Kedyrn; a meuyl ymi,'[15] heb ef, 'ony cheissaf i waret rac hynn.' Ac ymedyryaw ymlith[16] calaned y Gwydyl, a dyuot deu Wydel uonllwm idaw, a'y uwrw yn y peir yn rith Gwydel. Emystynnu idaw ynteu yn y peir, yny dyrr[17] y peir yn pedwar dryll, ac yny dyrr[18] y galon ynteu.

Ac o hynny y bu y meint goruot a uu y wyr Ynys y Kedyrn. Ny bu oruot o hynny eithyr diang seithwyr, a brathu Bendi-

---

[1] gwneuthur. [2] herwyd y draet. [3] ac heb ohir kynn kael. [4] tan *added*. [5] phan. [6] Branwenn.
[7] gyngytywys. [8] ymgyuoc. [9] niuer. [10] yny.
[11] y. [12] daryan. [13] drannoeth. [14] yn gystal. [15] ym.
[16] ym plith. [17] *and* [18] tyrr.

BRANWEN UERCH LYR

geiduran yn y troet a guenwynwaew. Sef seithwyr a dienghis,¹
Pryderi, Manawydan, Gliuieu² Eil Taran, Ta-(57)lyessin, ac
Ynawc, Grudyeu uab Muryel, Heilyn uab Gwyn Hen.   390

Ac yna y peris Bendigeiduran llad y benn. 'A chymerwch
chwi y penn,' heb ef, 'a dygwch hyt y Gwynuryn yn Llundein,
a chledwch ³a'y wyneb ar Freinc ef.³ A chwi a uydwch ar y
ford yn hir; yn Hardlech y bydwch seith mlyned ar ginyaw,
ac Adar Riannon y canu ywch. A'r penn a uyd kystal 395
gennwch y gedymdeithas ac y bu oreu gennwch, ban⁴ uu arnaf
i eiryoet. Ac y Guales ym Penuro y bydwch pedwarugeint
mlyned. Ac yny agoroch y drws parth ac Aber Henueleu,⁵ y tu
⁶ar Gernyw,⁶ y gellwch uot yno a'r penn yn dilwgyr genhwch.
Ac o'r pan agoroch y drws hwnnw, ny ellwch uot yno. 400
Kyrchwch Lundein y gladu y penn. A chyrchwch chwi racoch
drwod.' Ac yna y llas y benn ef, ac y kychwynassant a'r penn
gantu⁷ drwod, y seithwyr hynn,⁸ a Branwen yn wythuet. Ac y
Aber Alau⁹ yn Tal Ebolyon y doethant y'r tir. Ac yna¹⁰ eisted
a wnaethant, a gorfowys. Edrych oheni hitheu ar Iwerdon, ac 405
ar Ynys y Kedyrn, a welei ohonunt. 'Oy a uab Duw,' heb hi,
'guae ui o'm ganedigaeth. ¹¹Da a dwy ynys¹¹ a diffeithwyt o'm
achaws i.' A dodi ucheneit uawr, a thorri y chalon ar hynny.
A gwneuthur bed petrual¹² idi, a'e chladu yno yGlan Alaw.

Ac ar hynny, ker-(58)det a wnaeth y seithwyr parth a Hard- 410
lech, a'r penn ganthunt. Val y bydant y¹³ kerdet, llyma gyweithyd yn kyuaruot ac wynt, o wyr a gwraged. 'A oes gennwch
chwi chwedleu?' heb y Manawydan. 'Nac oes', heb wynt, 'onyt
goresgyn o Gaswallawn uab Beli Ynys y Kedyrn, a'y uot yn
urenhin coronawc yn Llundein.' 'Pa daruu,' heb wynteu, 'y 415
Gradawc¹⁴ uab Bran, a'r seithwyr a edewit y gyt ac ef yn yr ynys
honn?' 'Dyuot Caswallawn am eu penn, a llad y chwegwyr, a

---

¹ dihengis.   ² Gliuieri.   ³ yno ef ae wyneb ar Freinc.
⁴ pan.   ⁵ R Henuelen *sic leg.*   ⁶ a Chernyw.   ⁷ gantunt.
⁸ hynny.   ⁹ Alaw.   ¹⁰ yno.   ¹¹ ys da dwy ynys.
¹² pedryual.   ¹³ yn.   ¹⁴ Garadawc (*but* Gradawc *below*).

thorri ohonaw ynteu Gradawc y galon o aniuyget,[1] am welet y
cledyf yn llad y wyr, ac na wydat[2] pwy a'e lladei. Caswallawn
a[3] daroed idaw wiscaw llen hut amdanaw, ac ny welei neb ef
yn llad y gwyr, namyn y cledyf. Ny uynhei[4] Gaswallawn y lad
ynteu: y nei, uab y geuynderw, oed. A hwnnw uu y trydyd dyn
a torres y gallon o aniuyget.[5] Pendarar Dyuet, a oed yn was
ieuang gyt a'r seithwyr, a dienghis[6] y'r coet,' heb wynt.

Ac yna y kyrchyssant wynteu Hardlech, ac y dechreussant
eisted, ac y dechreuwyt ymdiwallu o uwyt a llynn. Ac y ⟨gyt
ac y[7]⟩ dechreuyssant wynteu uwyta ac yuet, dyuot tri ederyn,
a dechreu canu udunt ryw gerd, ac oc a glywssynt o gerd,
diuwyn oed pob un iwrthi hi. A fell[8] dremynt oed udunt [9]y
guelet uch benn[9] y weilgi allan.[10] (59) A chyn amlyket oed
udunt wy a chyn bydynt gyt ac wy. Ac ar hynny o ginyaw
y buant seith mlyned.

Ac ym penn y seithuet ulwydyn, y kychwynyssant parth a
Gualas ym Penuro. Ac yno yd oed udunt lle teg brenhineid uch
benn y weilgi, ac yneuad uawr[11] oed,[12] ac y'r neuad y kyrchyssant. A deu drws a welynt[13] yn agoret; y[14] trydyd drws oed[15] y[16]
gayat, yr hwnn y[17] tu a Chernyw. 'Weldy racco,' heb y Manawydan, 'y drws ny dylywn ni y agori.' A'r nos honno y buant yno
yn diwall, ac yn digrif ganthunt. Ac yr a welsynt o ouut[18] yn y
gwyd, ac yr a gewssynt[19] e hun, ny doy[20] gof udunt wy[21] dim,
nac o hynny nac o alar yn y byt. Ac yno y treulyssant y pedwarugeint mlyned hyt na wybuant wy[22] eiryoet dwyn yspeit
digriuach na hyurydach no honno. Nyt oed anesmwythach,
nac adnabot o un ar y gilyd y uot yn hynny o amser, no fan[23]

---

[1] annyuyget.   [2] wydyat.   [3] ar.   [4] mynnei.
[5] niuyget.   [6] dihengis.   [7] *Emendation supplied by Sir Ifor Williams*, PKM.   [8] phell.   [9] eu gwelet uch penn.
[10] *Here the scribe of* W *began to copy the next sentence but one*—'ac ar hynny o'—*and then scored these words out.*   [11] a *added*.
[12] yno udunt *added*.   [13] oed.   [14] ar.   [15] *Omitted*.
[16] yn.   [17] *Omitted*.   [18] vwyt.   [19] glywys.   [20] doey y *sic leg.*   [21] hwy.   [22] hwy.   [23] phan.

BRANWEN UERCH LYR

doethan[1] yno. Nit oed anesmwythach ganthunt wynte[2] gyduot 445
y penn yna, no phan uuassei Uendigeiduran yn uyw gyd ac
wynt. Ac o achaws y pedwarugeint mlyned hynny y gelwit
Yspydawt Urdaul Benn. (Yspydawt Uranwen a Matholwch oed
yr honn yd aethpwyt e Iwerdon).*

Sef a wnaeth Heilyn uab Guyn dydgueith: 'Meuyl ar uy 450
maryf[3] i,' heb ef, 'onyt agoraf y (60) drws, e wybot ay gwir a
dywedir am hynny.' Agori y drws a wnaeth, ac edrych ar
Gernyw, ac ar Aber Henueleu.[4] A phan edrychwys, yd oed yn
gyn hyspysset ganthunt y gyniuer collet a gollyssynt eiryoet,
a'r gyniuer car a chedymdeith a gollyssynt, a'r gyniuer drwc 455
a dothoed[5] udunt, a chyt bei yno[6] y kyuarffei ac wynt; ac yn
benhaf oll[7] am eu harglwyd. Ac o'r gyuawr honno, ny allyssant
wy orfowys namyn ky⟨r⟩chu[8] a'r penn parth a Llundein. Pa
hyt bynnac y bydynt ar y ford, wynt a doethant hyt yn
Llundein, ac a gladyssant y penn yn y Gwynuryn. 460

A hwnnw ⟨uu y[9]⟩ trydyd matcud [10]ban gudywyt,[10] a'r trydyd
anuat datcud pann datcudywyt; cany doey ormes byth drwy
uor y'r ynys honn, tra uei y penn yn y cud hwnnw. A hynny a
dyweit y kyuarwydyd hwnn.[11] Eu kyfranc wy,[12] 'Y gwyr a
gychwynwys o Iwerdon' yw hwnnw. 465

En Iwerdon nyt edewit dyn byw, namyn pump gwraged
beichawc ymywn gogof yn diffeithwch Iwerdon. A'r pump
wraged[13] hynny, yn yr un kyfnot, a anet udunt pum[14] meib.
A'r pym[15] meib hynny a uagyssant hyt ban[16] uuant weisson
mawr, ac yny uedylyssant am wraged, ac yny uu damunet 470
gantunt eu cafael. Ac yna, kyscu pob un lau heb lau (61) gan
uam y gilid, a gwledychu y wlat a'y chyuanhedu, a'y rannu y

---
[1] doethant. [2] wynteu. [3] maraf. [4] R Henuelen
sic leg. [5] dathoed. [6] yna. [7] *Omitted*. [8] W
reads kychu, R kychwynnu. [9] *Supplied from* R. [10] pan
cudywyt. [11] *Omitted*. [12] hwy. [13] gwraged. [14] pump.
[15] pump. [16] pan.

* Brackets used editorially to indicate that the sentence is in parenthesis.

¹rydunt yll pymp.¹ Ac o achaws y ranyat hwnnw y gelwir ²etwan pymp rann Ywerdon.² Ac edrych y wlat a wnaethant ford y buassei yr aeruaeu, a chael eur, ac aryant, yny ytoedynt yn gyuoethawc.

A llyna ual y teruyna y geing honn o'r Mabinyogi,³ o achaws Paluawt Branwen, yr honn a uu tryded anuat paluawt yn yr ynys honn; ac o achaws⁴ Yspadawt Uran,⁵ pan aeth ⁶yniuer pedeir decwlat⁶ a seithugeint e Iwerdon, y dial Paluawt Branwen; ac am y ginyaw yn Hardlech seith mlyned; ac am Ganyat Adar Riannon; ac a⟨m⟩⁷ Yspydaut Benn pedwarugeint mlyned.

[1] ryngtunt ell pump. [2] ettwa pump rann Iwerdon.
[3] Mabinogi. [4] achas. [5] Bran. [6] niuer deg wlat.
[7] W *and* R *read* ar.

NOTES

1. *Bendigeiduran*: i.e. Bendigeid+Brân, 'Blessed Brân'. The second element of the compound is lenited, and the accent falls, regularly, on *-eid-*. This accentuation occasionally caused the loss of the *-f-* or len. *-b-* of the second element of the compound, giving rise to forms such as *Bendigeidran* (WG 57, 179). The name seems to be a monkish 'improvement' on the simple form *Brân*. But *Bendigeid* may be used euphemistically, to flatter one who was in origin a malefic deity, according to Krappe (28). Rachel Bromwich, however, suggests that the 'original epithet was composed from *Pen* (head) with a following adjective', referring to Brân's severed head (Loomis, *Arthurian Literature in the Middle Ages*, 51).

The tradition which makes Llŷr the father of Bendigeidfran and of Branwen is probably a late one. Llŷr is rather the father of Manawydan, cf. Irish Manannán mac Lir.

a oed urenhin coronawc: 'was a crowned king'.

2. *ardyrchawc* < *ar-* 'before', 'in front of' +*dyrch* (derch)+*-og* adj. suffix. *dyrch* is from the root **derk* 'see', which appears in *drych* 'aspect', 'appearance', *edrych* 'to look'. Cf. O.Ir. *airdirc* 'famous'. *ardyrchawc o* 'famed for, adorned with'. GPC suggests 'invested with'.

W. J. Gruffydd, in Cymm. Trans. 1912–13, 56 and 64, follows Rhŷs in regarding the phrase *ardyrchawc o goron Lundein* as unidiomatic Welsh, owing something to the Latinity of Geoffrey of Monmouth, whose *Historia Regum* was written *c.* 1139. Although this usage with *o* is not an isolated instance, the argument has some force. This is one of several indications that *Branwen* may have been subjected to some alteration in the twelfth century.

Lundein: the radical form of the word, *Llundein*, is here lenited, after the fem. noun *coron*.

prynhawngueith: *pryt*+*nawn*+*gweith*, lit. 'time of noon once upon a time', i.e. 'one afternoon'. The word has an adverbial force.

3. *Ardudwy*: the name of a commot, i.e. neighbourhood or district, on the north-eastern shore of Cardigan Bay. It stretched from the Ffestiniog valley in the north to the Mawddach estuary in the south, and within its bounds was Harddlech (modern Harlech). See HW 238.

yn llys idaw: 'at a court of his'. In Mod. W. *mewn*, not *yn*, would be used with an indefinite noun, as l. 56, *ymywn ty*. See WG 416. For a similar instance, see *yn dadleu idaw* (232).

4. *weilgi*: mut. of *gweilgi* (1) 'the sea', 'the deep sea', (2) a 'stormy sea', 'heavy sea'. The word seems to be cognate with Ir. *fáelchú* 'wolf', and it is a metaphorical term, or kenning, for the sea. A further possibility is that the first element is *gwael* in the sense of 'wild'. See G 601, 647.

NOTES

5. *broder*: dual and pl. of *brawt*. Later affected to *brodyr*. In Med. W. *brodorion* is also used, often in the sense of 'kinsmen', 'fellow countrymen'. In late Med. W. this came to mean 'natives', and *brodor* 'a native' is a new sg. 'deduced from this pl.' (WG 209).

Un uam: *un* here forms a loose compound with the noun *mam*, leniting it. Transl. 'having the same mother'.

8. *Penardun*: 'fair' or 'beautiful (*arddun*) head'. But I.W. suspects that the original form of the woman's name may have been *Garddun*. She may originally have been the sister rather than the daughter of Beli Mawr. See Rachel Bromwich's article in *Studies in Early British History* 103 n. 5. Also *Welsh People* 39 n.

Ueli uab Mynogan: the name *Beli* has been equated with the Ir. name *Bile*. An interesting correspondence occurs between an entry in the *Annales Cambriae*, s.a. 722, recording the death of Beli son of Elfin, and one in the *Annals of Ulster*, s.a. 721, where the form is Bile mac Eilphin, King of Alcluath. Sir John Rhŷs went on to identify Beli with the Ir. Balor (HL 318 n.). T. F. O'Rahilly (EIHM 67) suggested that Beli may be the Welsh development of Celtic *Belgios or *Bolgios, and that the spear sometimes associated with him may be compared to the Ir. *gaí Bulga*. The name Mynogan may well be fictitious or out of context here, but similar forms are known from other sources (SEBH, loc. cit.).

For the len. of *Ueli* and *uab*, see Introd. xiv.

9. *ef a barei tangneued y rwg y deu lu*: the direct object of a verb is usually lenited: thus the reading of R, *dangneued*, indicates the len. R reads *y deulu*, which might be translated 'his family (retinue)'. The reading of W, however, makes better sense. It could refer to the two factions of (1) the family of Llŷr, represented by Bendigeidfran and Manawydan, and (2) the family of Eurosswyd, represented by Nissyen and Efnyssyen. On the other hand, the ref. to *y deu uroder*, i.e. Bendigeidfran and Manawydan, is against this interpretation. Since the def. art. is sometimes used 'indefinitely', perhaps the correct sense is that Nissyen made peace 'between two armed hosts when they were most enraged' whereas Efnyssyen caused strife between two brothers when they were most amicable.

10. *sef*: see Introd. xviii. A detailed discussion of constructions with *sef* in Med. W. is given in *Bull*. xviii, Pt. 1, 38.

13. *wynt*: the common form is *wy*. The *-nt* termination is borrowed from the 3 pl. ending of the verb.

15. *a cherdet rugyl*: *cerdet* (cerdded) can be used in several senses, meaning sometimes 'walking', &c., but here referring to the ships' motion. See GPC, *cerdded, cerddaf*, 1 (*c*)='to sail', 'navigate'. *rhugl* is used in Mod. W. in the sense of 'free' or 'fluent *of speech*'.

18. *wiscaw*: len. form of *gwiscaw* 'arm'.

pa uedwl yw yr eidunt: lit. 'what thought is theirs'. The poss.

pronouns are sometimes used thus substantivally with the art., cf. *arnaf i ac ar y meu* 'on me and on mine'; *yr eidaw* (*ef*) 'his', ll. 35, 91.

20. *y wayret*: 'downwards'. Bendigeidfran's men go down the slope (or cliff) to sea-level to meet those approaching in the ships. *gwayret* (gwaered) means 'a descent', 'slope', cf. the Ir. and Sc. G. usage *i bhfán* (Mod. Sc. G. *a bhán*) 'down' from *fán* 'a slope'. In the opposite sense Welsh has a similar usage: *y uyny*[*d*] 'upwards' (< *mynydd* 'mountain'), l. 25.

21. *gyweirach*: compar. of *kyweir* (cywair) 'prepared', 'well-ordered'. A compar. adj. is regularly lenited when it occurs in a neg. or interrogative sentence.

22. *arwydon*: pl. of *arwyd*(*d*) 'banner', 'ensign'.

arwreid: *arwr* 'hero'+-*eidd* adj. termination. I. W. compares the two senses of Eng. 'brave', 'bravery'.

pali: 'silk', 'brocaded silk'. A loanword from Fr. *paile*.

23. *nachaf*: 'behold!' I. W. has suggested that this word is composed of an interr. part. and a form (presumably pres. 1 sg.) of a W. cognate of Ir. *ad-cíu* 'I see'.

25. *swch*: 'point', 'plough-share', 'snout'. The Gael. cognate *soc* has the same senses.

26. *ymglywynt*: the prefix *ym*- usually implies a mutual action or process.

bwrw: '(they) put'. *Bwrw* is a flexible word, used idiomatically in various contexts, e.g. *bwrw eira* 'to snow'.

28. *e*: an older spelling of the def. art. *y*.

a'e ... wynteu: *e* is the inf. pron. 3 pl. This pron. is reinforced by the conjunctive form *wynteu*.

29. *rodo*: the pres. subj. used to express a wish. R here has the older spelling *rodho*, containing the once characteristic -*h*- of the subj., the len. form of older -*s*-. 'May God prosper you'.

30. *grayssaw*: Forms of this word occur with initial *c*- and initial *g*-. The *g*- in this instance is not the mut. of *c*-.

pieu: 'whose is?' 'to whom belongs?' In some contexts, e.g. l. 32, *pieu* can be translated 'owns'. The word is composed of the dat. form of the interr. pron.+*eu*, a variant form of *yw*, pres. 3 sg. of the verb 'to be'. The verb probably did not build up a complete conjugation, but many forms are known, e.g. imperf. 3 sg. *pioed*(*d*), fut. 3 sg. *pieifydd*, perf. 3 sg. *pieivu*, &c. *pieu* and *pioed* are the primary forms. See WG 357.

yniuer < Lat. *numerus*. An unstable *y* developed before certain Lat. loan-words with initial *n*- or *s*- plus a consonant. *nifer* eventually becomes the common form (cf. 62). But *y* (*e*, *a*) also developed before some native words, e.g. *yneuad* (127). The reading of R, *y niuer llongeu*, may well be preferred here.

yssyd: the rel. form of the pres. 3 sg. of the verb 'to be' used as a copula. It is composed of *ys* and *yd* (*ydd*), orig. the rel. part.

31. *mae*: used at the beginning of the clause and foll. by the predicate *ymma*.

NOTES

32. *bieu*: *pieu* is lenited because it is used in a rel. construction, although the rel. part. or pron. is not expressed here (94 n.). The rel. is not required before *pieu*. See WG 358. The copula is to be understood in the first phrase, *ac ef.* Transl. 'and it is he who owns the ships'.

32–33. *Beth ... a uynnhei ef? A uyn ef ...?*: 'What might he want? Does he want ...?'

33–35. The sense is: 'He does not wish to land unless his errand succeeds; he has business with you'. The phrase *negessawl yw wrthyt ti* is out of sequence.

Na uynn: *na* is the form of the neg. part. used in answering a question.

neges: < Lat. *necesse* 'what is necessary', hence 'business, errand'.

35. See l. 18 n.

36. *ymgyuathrachu*: (ym-cyf-athr-ach-u). *ym-* reflex. pref.; *cyf-* has the force of 'together'; *athr* : Lat. *inter* (cf. *athrywyn* 'intervention', 'arbitration' < Lat. *intervenio*, or from *athr-*, *ethr-*+an unknown element (GPC 237)); *ach* 'relationship', 'lineage', 'pedigree'; *-u* verbal suffix. The word implies the uniting of two families by marriage.

38. *Ynys y Kedeirn*: 'The Island of the Mighty (Ones)' (< *cadarn* 'strong'), i.e. Britain.

gadarnach: the adj. used predicatively after parts of the verb *bot* is often lenited (GCC § 18).

39. *chynghor*: with *kynghor* 'counsel', &c. cf. Ir. *cogar* < *com-cor* 'a putting together'. This develops the senses (1) 'a conference', (2) 'a whisper'. Cf. Sc. G. *cagar* 'whisper'.

45–46. *tryded prif rieni*: *tryded(d)* is the fem. form of the ordinal *trydyd(d)*. It is commonly used in the Welsh stories and triads in the sense of 'one of the three'. There is a similar Ir. usage, e.g. *in treas sét is ferr fuair Find riam* 'one of the three best treasures Find ever got', *Acal.* l. 20.

46. *rieni*: Zimmer connected the word with *rhiain* 'maiden', 'virgin', and used this instance to support his theory of matriarchy. I. W. prefers Vendryes's suggestion that the word derives from *rhy-geni*, i.e. 'born before'. It seems to be used in the sense of 'ancestor'. The three ancestors may have been Rhiannon as the mother of Pryderi, Branwen as the mother of Gwern, and Aranrhod as the mother of Leu Llawgyffes. Branwen, however, was not an ancestor, or ancestress, at this point in the story; this is one of several instances of anachronisms introduced by the 'editor' of the Mabinogi.

There is the further complication that later in the tale the only son we know Branwen to have had was killed as a boy. Rachel Bromwich suggests that Branwen was included in the triad of the three ancestors because she is a descendant of the ancestor *par excellence*, Beli Mawr (SEBH 104).

Thomas Jones in an article in *Bull.* ix, 131, points out that *rieni* can also be used in the sense of 'descendant', but that is not likely to be the sense here.

47. *Aberfraw*: this was the chief court of the princes of Gwynedd, the northern Welsh kingdom. Aberffraw is situated in Anglesey.

52. *dechreu . . . eisted*: the vn. is frequently used in a finite sense. Sometimes the appropriate tense of *gwneuthur* 'to make', 'do' is used as an auxiliary, as in ll. 58–59. See Introd. xvi.

54–55. *Branwen uerch Lyr*: Llyr is lenited after the fem. *merch*, which is itself lenited since it stands in apposition to Branwen; cf. also l. 95. Contrast, in the previous line, *Manawydan uab Llyr*.

56. *palleu*: *pall*, used here in the sense of 'tent', is a borrowing of Lat. *palla*, which meant 'a long and wide upper garment of the Roman ladies', and also 'a curtain'. The sense of 'covering' develops, then that of 'tent'. I. W. compares the Eng. expression 'under canvas'.

57. *angassei*: pluperf. 3 sg. of the verb (*g*)*enni*. This verb occurs both with and without initial *g*-. *genni* is probably the original form, but a new vn. *eingaw* was formed, under the influence, perhaps, of the vn. *eng*(*h*)*i* 'go out', 'escape'. The form *gein* occurs for the pres. ind. 3 sg. (R 1055. 26); this later became *geing*, and the *-ng-* spread to other forms of the verb, cf. *enghis* (317), *geingho* (318v.). See I. W., *Cyfranc Lludd a Llevelys* 32, and GCC § 165.

59. *uot*: mut. of *bot*, often used in this way to introduce an indirect statement after a verb of saying, &c.

60–61. The formalities of marriage in these tales consist of naming a time, usually a year or a year and a day in advance, celebrating a wedding feast, and co-habiting.

63. *rannyat*: 'billeting', 'quartering'. An abstract noun formed from *ran* (rhan) 'part'. The usage is similar to that of Eng. 'quartering'.

64. *kyueir*: 'region', 'place', 'spot'; cognate with Ir. *comair*, as in *ar comair*, *fo chomair* 'opposite', Mod. Gaelic *fa chomhair*. The word is used in a similar way in Mod. W. *ar gyfair* (*ar gyfer*). The O.W. form *arcimeir* occurs in the Computus fragment.

66. *dywanu y*: 'to happen upon', 'come on'. The prep. *ar* is more usual than *y* in this context. The verb is a compound of *gwanu* 'strike'; cf. *taro ar* 'happen upon', 'meet by chance'.

meirch: the spelling *meirych* occurs in l. 63 and elsewhere, indicating the presence of a svarabhakti vowel in the spoken word. The scribe of R, however, uses the form *meirch* fairly consistently. Both scribes use svarabhakti spellings of a number of other words, exx. from the text of W being *anfuryf* (76), *cenedyl* (83), *kynnedyf* (139), *trachefyn* (224), *sugyn* (287), *llestyr* (287), *ehegyr* (311), *colouyn* (329), *meuyl* (381), *keuynderw* (422), *maryf* (rad. *baryf*) (451). An instance in which R has the svarabhakti form where W has not occurs in l. 255: R *amylhawys*, W *amlawys*. The R spelling in this last instance is due to the simplex *amyl*.

69. *yr*: see l. 80 n.

70. *chwaer*: the *w* is written suprascript in W. Did this influence R's form, or does it suggest a common original without internal *w*?

72. *uwy*: see l. 21 n.

73. *guan y dan y meirych*: 'he struck up at the horses'. *y dan*, lit. 'from below', 'under'. The phrase is literally descriptive, and it seems unnecessary to find idiomatic usages of *gwanu y dan* to explain it otherwise.

74. *wrth*: 'close to'.

danned: pl. of *dant* (Ir. *dét*). Some old neut. nouns form pl. with *-ed(d)* or *-oed(d)*; occasionally with vowel mut. as well: *dant, dannedd, deint* (later used as sg.); *dwfyr, dyfredd, deifyr*; *môr, moroedd, mŷr*.

75. *rawn*: used for long coarse hair, and particularly horse-hair: Ir. *rón* 'horse-hair'; Sc. G. *ròin*, diminutive *ròineag* 'a hair'. Cf. a similar phonetic correspondence in the word for 'peat', Sc. G. *mòine*: W. *mawn*.

ny caei graf: 'where he could get a grip, catch'. *ny* = *yn y* or *lle y*. It has been suggested (see Mac Cana, *Branwen Daughter of Llŷr* 158–9) that the passage describing the mutilation of the horses may be based on a similar passage in the Latin *Life of St. Cadoc*, composed late in the eleventh century.

80. *yr*: R omits this, using simply the rel. construction with *a*. *Yr*, a variant form of the preverbal part. *ry*, is sometimes used as a rel. part. (see GCC. § 60 n. 2). The rel. pron. *a/y* came to be placed before *ry/yr*, hence *a ry, ar, y ry, yr ry*. W, using both *yr* and *a*, seems to confuse the two constructions. In 69 *yr* seems to be used in the same way as *ry* perfective.

83. *kyuurd*: (cyf-urdd) 'of such high rank'. Eq. adjs. are in many cases formed from nouns by adding the prefix *cym-, cyn-, cyf-*, or *cy-*, e.g. *kyvoet* 'of the same age', *cymaint* 'of the same size'.

84. *ti a wely dangos ef*: the sense of this phrase is perhaps clearer than its syntax. It seems to mean 'you shall see it is obviously so', i.e. the speaker assures Matholwch that the only interpretation of previous events is that he (Matholwch) is being deliberately insulted. *ef* is sometimes in earlier usage equivalent to 'so'. I. W. suggested various emendations:

(1) *y dangos ef* (*y = ei* 'its') lit. 'its showing' = 'the showing of it',
(2) *dangos mae ef* (the reading of R),
(3) *dangos os ef* 'if it is that'.

I. W. inclines to (3), interpreting the situation thus: the first friend thinks that the insult is intentional; Matholwch cannot believe this in view of his being given Branwen to wife; the second friend says that he will have further proof or demonstration (*dangos*) if the theory of the first friend is correct.

But *dangos* can also mean 'declare', so the phrase may be translated 'you see it being made plain'.

84–85. *nyt oes it a wnelych*: 'there is nothing you may do'. *gwnelych* is the pres. subj. 2 sg. of *gwneuthur*, the subj. being used here after the general antecedent *a*.

NOTES

90. *godiwawd*: perf. 3 sg. of *godiwes*. R has the form *gordiwedawd*, perf. 3 sg. of *gordiwes*, but formed by adding *-awd* to the pres. stem *gordiwed-*. See WG 338.

92. *Dioer* < *Duw a ŵyr*: lit. 'it is God who knows' (WG 452).

pei ys gwypwn: *pei* is the petrified imperf. subj. 3 sg. of *bot*, used in the sense of 'if'. *ys* (*as*) is the form of the inf. pron. 3 sg. used after certain conjunctions, e.g., *can*, *kyt* (*cyd*) &c. *gwypwn* is used here, as often, in the sense of a pluperf. subj. (and similarly with *down*). Transl. 'if I had known it' (or 'that').

94. *A reuedawt rygyueryw a mi*: 'and it is a strange thing that has happened to me'. Note that the rel. part. is not expressed: this is the older construction. *kyueryw* is perf. 3 sg. of *cyfarfod* (cf. *deryw* and *darfod* for a similar development). The scribe of R, writing *rygynneryw*, has a form *cyn+darfod (*cynnarfod*) in mind. See WG 353.

95. *Bronwen*: although the name (White-breast) is eminently suitable for a heroine, this isolated ex. of it may be simply the interpolation of a second hand. But Mac Cana suggests (155) that this may be the older form, which was later assimilated to the name Brân.

105. *ymchwelwys*: notice the sg. verb, used after a pl. subject. But R has a pl. verb *ymchoelassant*. See Introd. xv.

107. *nyt oes ymwaret e uynet*: R reads *oe uynet*, which gives good sense, lit. 'there is no deliverance from his going', i.e. we cannot prevent his going.

108. *nys*: the neg. *ny* combined with the inf. pron. 3 sg., *s*.

111. *ef a geif . . . .*: This statement borders on *oratio recta*. *ef a* probably corresponds to the affirm. particle. *fe* in Mod. W. is normally used in a direct statement.

112. *am pob*: the reading of R is *am bob*, which indicates the correct mut. after *am*.

113. *wynepwerth*: 'honour-price', 'compensation for insult'. R reads *wynebwarth*, making the second element of the compound *gwarth* 'disgrace', 'reproach'. This may be one of several instances of unsuccessful 'editing' on the part of the Red Book scribe. The form of W is supported, *inter alia*, by the O.Bret. form *enep-uuert* from the Cartulary of Redon, and by the Ir. *enech-log*. The primary sense of *wyneb* is 'face', with a secondary development to 'honour'.

llatheu: R's reading gives *u* mistakenly for *n*. It is probably not intended as the pl. of *llath*.

a'e uys bychan: this is supplied by I. W. in his edn. of *Branwen* (PKM 33 and notes 175). I. W. adduces evidence from the Welsh Laws regarding compensation. In the case of the King of Aberffraw this consisted of '100 cows from every cantref in his lordship, and a golden rod as tall (long) as himself, and as thick as his little finger (*a chyn frased a'i fys bychan*), together with a golden platter as broad as his face, and as thick as the nail of a husbandman of seven years' standing'.

In the Demetian Code the thickness of the golden rod is defined thus: *cyn frased a'i hirfys* 'as thick as his long finger'. The Gwentian Code says the rod must be *kyureuet ae arianuys* 'as thick as his "silverfinger"', and in passing an interesting survival in Sc. G. lore may be mentioned here: the little finger is still referred to in a folk-rhyme as *Màiri bheag an airgid* 'little Mary of the silver', possibly a corruption of *meur bheag an airgid* 'the little silver-finger', which would provide a parallel to Welsh *arianfys*. (But it should be noted that I. W. casts doubt on the reading *arianfys*, PKM, 177). The laws of compensation were sufficiently rigid, and sufficiently well-known, to make the reading of W and R here unlikely. There can be no question of Bendigeidfran offering Matholwch a silver rod as thick and long as he himself was.

Gaidoz, however, in an article in Cymm. vol. 10, 1–11, adducing Indian instances of the practice of giving a rod of gold or silver as reparation, suggests that the original practice was to give the person's *weight* in gold or silver. He looks on the definition of the Welsh Laws as 'an extenuation and a decay of the old custom: it is no more "the price of the weight", it is a substitute for it . . .'.

114. *clawr*: here probably in the sense of 'plate' or 'platter'; cf. Ir. and Sc. G. *clár*, which also has both this restricted sense and the broader sense of 'surface', 'expanse'. The phrase given here was used as a formula; cf. the identical phrase, in different orthography, from the *Black Book of Chirk* 3. 8 (*c*. A.D. 1200)—*claur eur kefled ay huynep*. Cf. the Irish formula *comlethet a enech di or 7 argut* 'the breadth of his face of gold and silver' (LU 1549).

115. *a phan yw*: *panyw* 'that it is'.

124. *a uei uvy*: the repetition of this phrase is probably due to a slip on the part of the scribe of W. The reading of R (*gymeint* entered suprascript) may be an attempt to improve the sense, but the best emendation would be to omit the second *a uei uvy* completely.

126. *pebylleu*: *pebyll* is the old sg. form, and is a borrowing of Lat. *pāpilio*. It forms the regular pl. *pebylleu*. Later *pebyll* was regarded as a pl. form, and a new sg. *pabell* appears. What the distinction is between *pall* and *pabell* is not clear, if indeed any distinction is intended here.

131–3. *Ac nachaf yn ardiawc gan Uendigeituran yr ymdidan, ac yn drist, a gaei gan Uatholwch, a'y lywenyt yn wastat kyn no hynny*: 'And lo! the conversation that he had with Matholwch seemed to Bendigeidfran listless and sorrowful, for he had always been cheerful before that'. The syntax, particularly of the last clause, is characteristic of both Welsh and the Goidelic languages (cf. the similar usage with *agus*, *is* in Mod. Sc. G.). Both W and R read *yn ymdidan*, which does not make good sense in the context. Did the scribe of R, accepting the form *yn*, try to mend the sentence by adding *am y warth* ('because of the reproach') after *drist*? This emendation might have been more successful had the roles of Bendigeidfran and Matholwch been reversed, but it was, of course, Matholwch who suffered reproach from Bendigeidfran.

I. W. notes two ways of interpreting *lywenyt*:
(1) with *t* = *dd*, giving *llywenydd* 'happiness',
(2) with *yt* = *et*, giving *llywenet*, eq. of *llawen*.

If we accept the second alternative, the transl. is 'so happy had he always been before that'. This seems less satisfactory either syntactically or with regard to the sense, but it is worth noticing that in the other two instances in this text when *llywenyd* occurs (with -*d*) it is the noun which is intended.

135. *un nos*: lit. 'one night'. The sense is 'the other night' or 'a night once upon a time'. The usage is not dissimilar to that of *uair* in Sc. G. *Bha mise uair nach b' e sud m' àbhaist* 'once upon a time that was not my wont' (Watson, *Gaelic Songs of Mary Macleod*, l. 501).

138. *delediwaf*: from *tal* 'value', we get *taladwy/telediw* 'of full value'. Hence the verb meaning 'fully recompense', perhaps developing the sense of 'augment' here.

139. *a chynnedyf y peir yw, y gwr . . .*: there is no proper logical sequence between *yw* and *y uwrw*. The sense is 'the cauldron has the characteristic (or magical quality) of making as good (i.e. fit) as ever . . . the man of thine who is slain today, if he is thrown into it'. Note that Gaelic *buaidh* is used in the same sense as *kynnedyf*.

peir: see Introduction, pp. xxxii–iii.

140. *erbyn*: the case-system as such had broken down before the time of the earliest manuscript writings in Welsh, but a few fossilized survivals bear witness to it, even in Mod. W. *erbyn* contains an oblique case (the dat.) of *pen(n)*, and the prep., in origin a compound one, corresponds morphologically to Ir. *ar chiund*, Sc. G. *air chionn*.

141–2. *diolwch a wnaeth ynteu hynny*: 'he gave thanks [for] that'.

144. *kymwt*: 'commot', 'province'; 'district', &c. The commot was a smaller unit than the cantref (two or more commots being included in the cantref), but it had a law-court of its own. See HW 300–1.

146. *Tal Ebolyon*: Talebolion and Twrcelyn were two commots of the cantref of Cemmais in Anglesey. See William Rees, *An historical atlas of Wales* 24–25, plate 28.

The story of the origin of the name is no doubt a piece of folk etymology. I. W. conjectures that the original form may have been *Tal y Bolion*, perhaps with the sense of 'the end of the deep cavities', or 'the end of the ridges'. But perhaps the name should be compared with Irish names such as Dún mBolg, Mag Bolg, &c. W. J. Gruffydd thought that the original onomastic tale may have explained *Tal y Bolion* by reference to *bolion* 'bags'; cf. the episode of the Irishmen in the bags. See Mac Cana 156–8.

150. *caffo*: pres. subj. 3 sg. of *caffael*, but here used with a perfective sense—'he may have found it'—as though it were preceded by the perfective part. *ry*. See IEW 58.

152. *ty hayarn*: see Introduction, xxxvi–xl.

153. *wenn*: if we accept this reading, the implication is that *ty* is here fem.; cf. also *burwen* in l. 157. It may well have been neut. originally, as *tech* was in Irish, and its later gender in Welsh may thus have been unstable. On the other hand, the instances we have here are scarcely sufficient to permit a firm conclusion, for *e* in W frequently stands for *y*, and the copyist may have omitted to modernize the orthography in these, as in other, instances; cf. *pethewnos* (164). The retention of the form *wenn*, qualifying the fem. noun *pleit* in l. 188, in close proximity to *burwen* qualifying *ty* (186), might perhaps be regarded as an indication that the scribe intended these as fem. forms, but this is doubtful.

159. *athrugar*: used here in the secondary sense of 'enormous' or 'loathsome'. Cf. the usage with *uamhasach* (*uathbhasach*) in Mod. Sc. G.

159–60. *drygweith anorles*: 'an evil unsightly aspect' (*gweith*) (?). Thomas Jones, however, suggests (*Bull.* xiii 74–75) that *anorles* should be emended to *anorlos*, for which he suggests the sense of 'warrior' or 'brigand'. He would analyse the word as follows: *an* intens. pref. + *gor* intens. pref. + *llos*, which he regards as a simplification of the form *lloes*, drawing attention to I. W.'s article (ZCP xxi 304) on the Breton glosses *loes* and *lois*. The phrase *a drygweith anorlos arnaw* would therefore mean 'with the evil look (appearance, guise) of a warrior (brigand) about him'.

164. *pethewnos*: the orig. meaning was 'fifteen nights'; cf. *pymtheg* 'fifteen'. There are still traces of an older method of counting days (or nights) in fives; cf. the common units of time in Sc. G. *deich là* 'ten days', *co'-là-deug* 'fifteen days', used for a fortnight, *fichead là* 'twenty days'. Cf. also Ir. *cóicthigheas* 'fortnight'.

167. *Y kymereis inheu wyntwy arnaf, yu gossymdeithaw*: 'I took them upon myself, to maintain them'. The primary sense of *gossymdeith* was 'provisions for a journey' (*ymdeith*). I. W. compares Lat. *viaticum*.

169. *y guarauunwyt im*: lit. 'they were grudged to me', i.e. Matholwch's subjects regarded the guests as an imposition on their king and his kingdom. *y* may here be regarded as containing both the particle *y* and the inf. pron. 3 pl. *y*. See GCC § 52.

169–70. *y pedwyryd mis*: 'the fourth month', i.e. of the second year.

170. *anghynwys*: see Vocab. Alternatively, used here as an adj., 'uncontainable', 'highly unwelcome' (?). *an-* neg. + *cynnwys* 'containing', cf. Ir. *éccendais*, adj., 'untamed', 'savage'.

171. *sarahedeu*: pl. of *sarhaed* (*sarhad*), which is used in two senses: (1) insult, act of violation, &c., (2) the fine paid for such offences. The word is used here in sense (1). The cognate technical term in Irish is *sárugud* (earlier *sárgud*), and it is used to mean 'the act of violating', 'dishonouring', 'outrage'. Sc. G. *sàrachadh*.

173. *ym = fym*, i.e. *fy + m* indicating nas. mut. of the foll. word. I. W. notes this as an early ex. of the loss of *f* in *fy*.

NOTES

175. *E dodeis inheu ar gynghor* . . .: lit. 'I placed on the council of my country what should be done about them', i.e. 'I left it to the council to decide, ...'

177. *herwyd ymlad*: lit. 'because of fighting', i.e. 'because of their fighting prowess (?)'. Prof. Dillon suggests 'by force'.

yn y kyuyng gynghor y causant . . .: the mut. of *kynghor* indicates that it is regarded as forming a virtual conpound with *kyuyng*, the compound meaning 'quandary', 'perplexity'. *cael* is used in conjunction with *kynghor* in the sense of 'decide', 'determine'.

kyuyng: *kyf-* (*cyf-*)+*yng* 'strait', 'distress'. For the form cf. O.Ir. *cumung*, Sc. G. *cumhang* 'narrow', &c. (L & P 34).

178. *y barawt*: the use of the predicative and adverbial particle *y* instead of *yn* is common in the text of W. The foll. adj. or noun is generally lenited; cf. *y dywyssogyon* (242), *y benhaf* (242), *y canu* (395), *y kerdet* (411), *y gayat* (436–7). See WG 439 and GCC § 18. Also *Bull.* xvii 137 ff. and xviii 362 ff.

179. *a oed o of* . . .: lit. 'what there was of smith'. Transl. 'all the smiths that there were'. Sim. *a oed o perchen* . . . .

o'r a oed . . .: lit. 'from what there was . . .'. (*'r* is from *ar*, demon. used as an antecedent: see WG 298–9, GCC § 70). The idea would seem to be that some kind of census was taken of possessors of tongs and hammers, and that the qualified smiths among them were then conscripted. R reads *o berchen geueyl a myrthwl*, (1) showing the mut. after *o*, (2) using the word for 'smithy' (*gefeil*) instead of that for 'tongs' (*gefel*), unless indeed *geueyl* and *myrthwl* are irregular pl. forms. The latter may well be the case; in the passage corresponding to PKM 63. 22 *mi a rodaf it a wely o uarch yn y maes hwnn*, RM 57. 1 has *o ueirch*.

181. *guassanaethu*: 'to serve'. Foll. by *ar* 'on'. Transl. 'they caused them—the woman, her husband, and her offspring—to be served abundantly with food and drink'.

182–3. *wybuwyt* . . . *dechreuwyt*: note the two impers. forms. But transl. 'when it was known . . . they began'.

186. *burwen*: see l. 153 n.

188. *wenn*: see l. 153 n.

193. *delw*: *w* here is consonantal, *delw* being therefore monosyllabic. *w* in Med. W. is usually non-syllabic after *d*, *dd*, *l*, *n*, *r* (WG 51).

194. This story is given as an explanation of the historical Irish settlements in Wales.

198. *llessach*: just as an eq. adj. is sometimes formed direct from a noun (83 n.), so too a compar. or superl. adj. can be formed from a noun. Here the noun is *lles* 'benefit', 'profit' (Gael. *leas*); cf. *pennaf*, *blaenaf*, &c. (WC 250).

199. *eisted a wei hwy*: lit. 'sitting that would be longer'. Transl. 'to sit (up) longer'.

201. *hynny*: 'these things'.

202. *A hynny*: 'and thereupon'. Similarly in ll. 213, 215.

I. W. suggests (PKM, 185) that *A hynny* here=*a'r rheini*. If we accept this the transl. is 'These thirteen ships set out . . .'.

Abermenei: Abermenai near Caernarvon was the principal port in N. Wales for sailing to Ireland. Its place, in this connexion, has been taken by Holyhead in Anglesey.

204-5. *(g)wr mawr*: 'great man', 'man of rank or substance'.

205-6. *ni rodei hi . . . ydaw*: 'to whom she did not give . . .'. See Introd. xx.

206. *cadwedic*: from the root *cadw* (as in the verb 'to keep') and the adj. suffix *-edic* (*-edig*).

208-9. *a hwyl delediw a duc hi o glot a chedymdeithon*: 'and she prospered with honour and friends'.

210. *amseroyd*: pl. of *amser* 'season'. 'After spending (passing) the due seasons, a son was born to her'.

212. *ar un lle goreu*: this is not satisfactory. R's reading *yr* =*i'r* '(in)to the' is to be preferred. Transl. 'to the very best place'.

213. *llyma* = *syll yma* 'look here!' (WG 440). An alternative derivation is from *a wely yman?* 'seest thou here?' (I. W., *Cyfranc Lludd a Llevelys* 9).

214. *somm*: the gender of this word is problematical. *heb y gelu* in l. 185 suggests that it is masc. here, but the phrase may refer to *guaradwyd* (m.). Mod. W. *siom* 'disgrace', 'shame', 'mockery' is fem.

216. *yn lliwaw idaw hynny*: 'taunting him with that'. *lliwaw* here has both a direct and an indirect object, *hynny* being the direct object in the Welsh idiom.

219-20. The punishment meted out to Branwen does not seem to bear any relation to her supposed crime. For a discussion of submerged layers of the story, here seen breaking the surface, see *Rhiannon*, especially 61-63. See also l. 478 n. (For a criticism of Gruffydd's reconstruction, see now Mac Cana 161 ff.).

222. *par weithon wahard*: 'cause (i.e. set) now an embargo (on)'.

223. *yscraffeu*: pl. of *yscraff* which is probably a borrowing from O.Icelandic *karfi* 'a swift-going ship', 'a galley' (cf. Ir. *carbh*). In the context it may refer to a medium-sized boat, not so large as a *llong*, nor so small as a *corwg*.

corygeu: *corwg* is the early form in the sg. (cf. Ir. *curach*). The Mod. W. form is *corwgl*, whence Eng. 'coracle'.

224. *na at*: the reading of R, *hyt nat elont* 'so that they may not go', is on the face of it the better one. But I. W.'s emendation *ac na at* makes good sense. *at* is impv.2 sg. of *gadu, gadael* 'let go'; cf. *ac nys gadwn* (108).

227. *ederyn drydwen*: lit. 'a bird of a starling'. This is a typical idiom in the other Celtic languages, cf. Sc. G. *beathach caorach* 'an animal of a sheep', i.e. one sheep. The idiom is less common in the pl. *Ederyn* is a singulative form (pl. *adar*) and *drydwen* is the diminutive of *drydw* > *drydwy*: Ir. and Sc. G. *druid*.

NOTES

229. *dwyn*: the sense is 'she brought a letter [with an account] of her woes ...' and tied it to the wing of the starling.

232. *Kaer Seint yn Aruon*: early forms are those of Nennius cc. 25, 66a, *Cair Segeint*, and Llywarch ap Llywelyn (Prydydd y Moch) 1173–1220, *Caer yn Arfon* (Llawysgrif Hendregadredd 276, 278). The old Roman fort was *Segontium* > *Segeint* > *Seint*. Modern derivatives are *Afon Saint, Pont Saint*.

236. *glybot*: mut. of *clybot*. The more usual form of the vn. is *clywed*.

237. *lle hwnnw*: *lle*, which is masc. in Mod. W., is recorded both as a masc. and a fem. noun in earlier Welsh; cf. *lle hon* (*Pwyll*, l. 58).

239. *wys*: mut. of *gwys* 'notice', 'summons'. Transl. here as 'levy'.

pedeir degwlat: notice how *deg* (= *deng*?) 'ten' enters into composition with the noun *gwlat*, and how *pedeir* (fem.) agrees with it in gender. The total count here is 154 districts (provinces), or 'seven score provinces and fourteen'. The count in R is different, *pedeir gwlat a seithugeint* (i.e. 144). (For *deg* > *deng*, see T. J. Morgan, *Y Treigladau a'u Cystrawen*, 135.)

240. *bot y poen a oed ar y chwaer*: lit. 'that there was the punishment which was on his sister', i.e. that his sister should endure the punishment she was enduring.

242. *y dywyssogyon* and *y benhaf*: *y* here = *yn*, used predicatively as a particle. R has *yn*. See l. 178 n.

243. *Edeirnon*: also called *Edeirnyawn, Edeirnion*, a commot once belonging to the kingdom of Powys, and traversed by the middle reaches of the Dee. It is named after Edern, son of Cunedda, the fifth-century king from the North who is traditionally credited with establishing supremacy over the greater part of N. Wales.

244. *Seith Marchawc*: cf. Bryn Saith Marchog between Ruthin and Corwen. Mac Cana (135–7) suggests that the traditions of Brân (> Bendigeidfran) were originally connected with north-east Wales (where there are place-names like Castell Dinas Brân, Gorsedd Frân, Llyn Brân), and that these traditions were 'later transplanted by some story-teller—the author of *Branwen*?—to the north-west'. Loth suggested that *Seith* here may be for *Sant* 'saint'. See PKM 191.

247. *Wlch Minasgwrn*: 'Wlch Bone-lip'. The description is sterner than that of the traditional English 'stiff upper lip', and is reminiscent of the names of Icelandic heroes of saga.

248. *Pendaran Dyuet*: see Introduction, xxiii–iv, xxix.

249–50. *kynueissat, kynweisyat*: *cynt-* + *gwas* + the agent suffix *-iad*, 'principal servitor' or 'steward'. The word occurs in one of the triads, where Caradawc son of Brân is named as one of the three principal stewards (*cynweissyat*) of Britain.

253. *yna*: with the colon before *yna* we would take the word in the sense of 'then', 'thereafter'. Punctuating with a colon after *yna* the sense would be 'then', 'at that time', i.e. the sea was not extensive at that time: he proceeded by wading. On the whole the second sense seems more suitable in the light of the next two sentences.

y ueis: Timothy Lewis, rejecting the marvellous element in the story (see note on 254–6), argued unconvincingly that *ueis* comes from a Scandinavian word for a fairly large ship (e.g. O.Icelandic *buza*), with three masts (*Mabinogi Cymru* 165). This must be rejected because (1) such an explanation is out of keeping with the context, and (2) the sense 'by walking', 'by wading' is satisfactory. Salesbury, in his Dictionary of 1547, gives *beisio dwfyr* in the sense of 'to wade'. *beis* or *bais* is used in the senses of 'stepping', 'walking'; 'bottom', 'ground', 'ford'; cf. *bas* 'shallow', 'fordable' (GPC). For this usage of *y* cf. *y dreis* 'by force'. Krappe pointed out (34) that the giant who crosses the sea by wading is common to Celtic, German, and Greek stories.

254–6. *A guedy hynny . . . tyrnassoed*: W. J. Gruffydd (Cymm. Trans. 1912–13, 62) regarded this whole sentence as a gloss added to the text. This view was confirmed, he said, by the fact that the Red Book copyist blundered over these words, omitting *pan oreskynwys y weilgi*. 'The words which he copied had been, without doubt, unskilfully crowded into the text.' Thomas Jones (*Bull.* xii 79 ff.) suggests that there are two glosses incorporated in this passage, and that these are inspired by stories of kingdoms that were inundated. He quotes a Latin triadic grouping which is presumably based on a lost Welsh triad. See also Mac Cana 109.

256. *a oed o gerd arwest*: lit. 'what there was of the craft of [instrument] strings'. In *Geirfa* it is suggested that the sense of *kerd arwest* may be 'stringed instruments'. *arwest*: lit. 'what is knotted or tied', 'the string', from the root **uedh-* 'bind', 'knit', 'tie', which is seen in *gwedd* 'yoke', O.Ir. *fedan*, Sc G. *feadhainn* (GPC 215).

258. *meicheit*: pl. of *meichiad* < *moch* 'swine' + the agent suffix *-iad*, which causes affection of the stem vowel.

259. *e dremynt*: *e* = *y*, the def. art. *dremynt* is a derivative of *drem* 'sight'. In the later language initial *t-* is more usual in both words.

261. *henpych guell*: lit. 'may you be better', a salutation which may more brusquely be translated 'Hail!' or 'Greetings!'

261–2. *a chwedleu genhwch*: *a* here can hardly be the interr. part.; the context seems to require a question, but the syntax is difficult. R resolves the difficulty by writing *a chwedleu y gennwch*, to be translated 'and stories from (*y gan*) you', i.e. 'let us have your news'. The lit. transl. of W's reading is 'and tidings with you'. For a Sc. Gael. parallel usage cf. *sgeula leat* (*Bàrdachd Ghàidhlig*, l. 5890).

269. *wypo*: mut. of *gwypo*, pres. subj. 3 sg. of *gwybot*. The subj. is used after an indef. antecedent.

271. *Kyn ny bwyf*: 'though I may not be (a lady)'.

NOTES

274. *gwernenni*: pl. of *gwernen* (with singulative *-en*) 'alder tree'; 'mast of ship'. Cf. Ir. *fern* 'alder'; *fern siúil* 'mast'.

275. *hwylbrenni*: pl. of *hwylbren* 'mast', 'yard-arm', lit. 'sail-tree'; cf. Ir. *crann-siúil*.

276. *gan ystlys*: 'by the side of'.

277. *y ueis*: see l. 253 n.

281. For a comment on ll. 265-81 see Introduction, xl-xlii.

282. *holl*: *holl* and *oll* may be regarded as positional variants, having the same function, either adjectival or adverbial. *oll* 'generally follows the word or phrase which it limits' (WG 309).—see ll. 178, 326, also 473 n.

285-6. *a gadu Llinon y rot ac ef*: 'and let Llinon be between you and him'. *Llinon*, the river Shannon, in Ir. *Sinann*. I. W. suggests that this form gives evidence of having been an oral, not a literary, loan. He regards the Welsh *ll* here as an attempt at reproducing the Ir. palatal *s*. But see Rachel Bromwich's criticism of this identification in *Medium Aevum*, xxviii, 208-9.

286-7. *mein sugyn*: lit. 'stones of suction', i.e. loadstones, which could draw a ship to the bottom.

287-8. *ny eill na llong na llestyr arnei* 'neither ship nor vessel can (be) on it'. *arnei* refers to the fem. noun *auon*.

290-1. *Bendigeiduran a doeth y'r tir, a llynghes y gyt ac ef, parth a glann yr auon*: Mac Cana (118 ff.) gives a valuable discussion of this passage. I. W. (PKM 196) had suggested that it shows a lack of knowledge of Irish geography on the part of the author, but Mac Cana shows that 'it is the story-teller's narrative that is deficient, not his geography'. 'It is,' he says, 'in all common sense, impossible to bring ships to land on the bank of a river and then find that the river is impassable for any vessel. In fact the only situation in which ships could come to the bank of the river would be where the river flowed out into the sea, in which case the difficulty of crossing it would be completely irrelevant.' Mac Cana proposes a solution by emending the text, and inserting a verb meaning 'to advance', 'proceed', before *parth a*. The progression of events then envisaged would be that Bendigeidfran landed on the east coast of Ireland, perhaps in the vicinity of Dublin, and followed the retreating Irish to the Shannon.

292. *mae*: here used in the sense of 'where is?'.

293-4. *a uo penn bit pont*: 'he who is head (i.e. leader), let him be a bridge'. This had become a proverbial saying, apparently, by the time the White Book was written.

295. *diharebir . . .*: the pres. impers. of the verb *diharebu, diarhebu*, based on *dihareb* 'a proverb'. Transl. 'people still use it as a proverb.

298. *Mallolwch* is the form in P: Rachel Bromwich draws attention to two instances of this form in the poetry of the *Gogynfeirdd*, and suggests that it may be the original form (review of Mac Cana in *Medium Aevum*, xxviii, 208).

301-2. *yn rodi brenhinaeth Iwerdon y Wern. . .*: Matholwch offers to abdicate in favour of his and Branwen's son, Gwern. W. J. Gruffydd (*Cymm. Trans.* 1912–13, 43) read more into this passage than is justifiable. He claimed that Matholwch offered Bendigeidfran 'these terms of peace—that Gwern should succeed to the Crown of Ireland after his own father Matholwch'. Gruffydd explained this gesture as an instance of inheritance through the female line—Gwern was Bendigeidfran's heir, not Matholwch's, and it was right that the conqueror should be succeeded by his proper heir. In the first place, it is misleading to say that Matholwch offered terms of peace. In the circumstances it is Bendigeidfran who is in a position to offer terms, as he fully realizes (306–7). What Matholwch is doing is making a bid for Bendigeidfran's friendship by doing honour to Branwen's son, and thus to Branwen and her brother Bendigeidfran. But see also Nora K. Chadwick's article 'Pictish and Celtic Marriage', *SGS* viii, 90.

304–5. *yn y lle y mynnych ditheu*: 'wherever you yourself desire'. The subjunctive is used in an indef. statement of this kind.

307. *ac aduyd*: this should probably be written as one word. Both this form and the simple verb *aduyd* (adfydd) are used, with a foll. verb, in the sense of 'perhaps'. This is a specialized usage of the fut. 3 sg. of the verb *adfod* (1) 'to pass away', 'vanish', (2) 'to happen', 'be'. The verb is not commonly used otherwise.

308. *O hyn hyt ban del amgen*: 'henceforth until different [terms] come', 'until a different answer comes'. *amgen* is here used as a noun. P expands the sense somewhat: the lit. transl. of P's reading is, 'From now until then you will not get an answer from me until there comes with you different from what has come'.

310. *yn*: Mod. W. *ein* 'our'.

312. *racdu*: lit. 'before them'. Transl. 'forward'. For a similar idiom cf. Sc. G. (*ghabh iad*) *rompa*, where *rompa* (3 pl.) is based on *roimh* 'before'.

313. *uo*: mut. of *bo*, pres. subj. 3 sg. of *bot*. It is used here with a potential sense.

318. *o'y*: $o < $ *do 'to'+inf. pron. 3 sg. The form *o'e* also occurs. Mod. W. has *i'w*. Transl. 'make (build) a house in his honour'.

320. *doro dy urenhinaeth yn y ewyllus*: lit. 'give your kingship into his will', i.e. place your kingship at his disposal. *doro* strictly belongs to a compound of *rhoddi*, namely *dy-rhoddi*, which is defective in most of its tenses. The prefix *dy-* survives in R's form *dyro*.

gwra: impv. 2 sg. of the verb *gwrhau* 'to do homage', 'become a vassal', 'become one's man'. It may be doubted, however, whether the term is used here in its proper feudal sense. See *Pwyll* xv.

321–2. *peth ny chauas eiryoet*: 'because he has never got'. I. W. regards this as an uncommon usage of *peth* as 'because' (PKM 199. See also GCC § 99 n. 2 and *Bull.* xvii 159). But it is syntactically possible to transl. *peth* literally—'a thing (something) he never had, a house that would contain him'. The construction is clumsy, but

NOTES

not uncharacteristic. R writes *nys kauas*, with the inf. *s* perhaps anticipating the foll. clause *ty a geinghei yndaw*. Instead of the spir. mut. after *ny*, P has lenition (*ny gafas*) as was common in relative clauses (see GCC § 60 n. 1).

326. *oed genti hitheu hynny*: lit. 'was that with her'. The sense is 'was that done by her' or 'was that counsel given by her'.

330. *boly croyn*: 'skin bag'. *boly* itself is used in the senses of 'belly', 'cavity'; 'swelling', 'bulge'; 'a hide or leather bag' (GPC 296). The word, which also has the forms *bol* and *bola*, is cognate with Ir. *bolg*. *boly* is monosyllabic, the *y* being the vestigial remnant of the final *g* (len.) which is retained in the Goidelic dialects. Another ex. is *hely* 'hunting' (Ir. *selg*), but the form used in our text (156) is *hela*.

332. *edrych golygon orwyllt*: lit. 'he looked fierce looks', i.e. he cast fierce glances. The lenition of (*g*)*orwyllt* is probably to be explained by regarding *golygon* as a dual form (as though referring to *deu lygat* 'two eyes'). Cf. l. 383.

335. *eneit*: lit. 'soul', but here in the sense of 'friend'. Cf. a similar usage (by preachers) of the Sc. G. *anam* 'soul'.

336–7. *yny glyw y uyssed yn ymanodi*: 'until he feels his fingers sinking into (penetrating)'. The *d* of *ymanodi* probably represents *dd*, while the *a* may be a svarabhakti vowel; cf. *ymnoddi*, or *ymnoeddi*. See Thomas Jones in *Bull.* x 133–4.

337. *ureithell*: the reading of P may be preferred. *Breithell* < *braith*, fem. of *brith* 'grey', 'speckled', used of the 'grey matter' of the brain (GPC 318). W has read *t* as *c*.

347–9. After he had killed the two hundred armed Irishmen in the bags, Efnyssyen gloatingly sang this englyn, which is translated in Jones (Everyman ed., 36) as follows:

'There is in these bags flour of a sort:
Champions, warriors, attackers in battle,
Against fighters, ready for the fray.'

There are two words *blawt* (blawd), one meaning 'meal', 'flour', 'powder', the other 'bloom', 'blossom'. The Irish had told Efnyssyen that the bags contained *blawt*, i.e. 'flour', but in the englyn he is probably punning on the word, and using it in the senses of (1) 'flour' > 'powder', and (2) 'blossom' > 'hero'. I. W., besides drawing attention to the second of these possibilities, suggests that by *blawt* Efnyssyen is referring to the various kinds of bread which the warriors ate when alive. This would involve a further pun on *boly* or rather on its pl. *byly* (see below), which can mean either 'bags' or 'bellies'. It is possible that he is punning also on the two senses of *amryw* (1) 'of a sort' (i.e. flour of a sort), (2) 'diverse', 'various' (referring to the warriors).

yssit: a form (3 sg.) of the copula, 'there is'.

boly hwnn: the reading *byly hyn* (pl.), suggests I. W., would be better, as Efnyssyen is now referring to the bags in general.

amryw: in the sense of 'various', 'several', used in Med. W. with a sg. noun (WG 303).

Mac Cana (64–71) regards the story of the bags as a possible borrowing from the *Bórama*. His argument is ingenious, but does not carry conviction.

349. *kydwyr*: pl. of *cadwr* 'warrior', 'man of battle' (*y* in first syllable = *e*).

cadbarawt: 'ready for the fray'. A compound epithet of the kind that is common in early Welsh poetry.

352. *gynebrwydet*: *cyn-ebrwyd(d)-et*; the eq. sense of the adj. is indicated by the use of *cyn-* and by the use of the suffix *-et*.

356. *a phawb o'r a'e guelei*: 'and all of those who saw him'.

358–9. *uy nei, uab uy chwaer*: *uab* is mut. because it is in apposition.

359–60. *Kyn ny bei urenhin . . . da oed genhyf*: 'though he were not king . . . I should like . . .'. *urenhin* is mut. foll. on a verb in the imperf. 3 sg. (similarly in the case of the pluperf.). Cf. *Ny uynhei Gaswallawn* (421). *oed* has a modal force, cf. *Ryuedawt hagen da oed gennyf pei ys gwelwn* (PKM 9. 9) 'A wonder, on the other hand, I should like to see it'.

362–3. *ys anhebic a gyflauan gan y tylwyth y wneuthur*: it may be worth following the syntax here in a bald word-for-word translation— 'it is [an] unlikely [kind] of an outrage by the household to do', i.e. it is an outrage that the household will not expect to be performed. Here *a* takes the place of the more usual *o*.

365. *yny*: two possible senses are (1) 'until'—'(he held the boy) until he thrust', (2) 'so that' (expressing purpose). Neither of these senses is altogether satisfactory in this context. *yny* here seems to have no conjunctive character; it is used as a preverbal affirmative prefix (see *Bull.* i 103 and GCC § 270 n.).

gwant: *t*-pret., 3 sg. of *gwanu*.

For a comment on the place of this episode (of throwing Gwern into the fire) in the story, see Mac Cana 77.

369. *ymgyuot o bawb*: 'everyone arose (sprang up)'. Lit. 'an arising from everyone'. This type of abrupt expression is not uncommon in passages of Med. W. prose, particularly in descriptions of swift action. Mac Cana (76) suggests that the scribe of R felt that the verb (*ymgyuot*) in his exemplar was too ambiguous, and substituted *ymgyuoc* (< *cyfogi* 'to fight'). Or he confused *c* and *t*, cf. l. 337.

371–2. *Guern gwn, gwchuiwch Uordwyt Tyllyon*: both W and R write *gwngwch uiwch*, and I. W. suggested the emendation given here. Transl. 'Hounds (i.e. warriors) of Gwern, beware of Morddwyd Tyllyon'. I. W. suggested that *gwchuiwch* was the impv. 2 pl. of a verb *gwchwyaf*, containing *-cwy-* from the same root as Lat. *caveo*. That such a challenge should be thrown out to the Irish (the warriors of Gwern, who had just perished in the flames) makes excellent sense in the context.

NOTES

W. J. Gruffydd, however, suggested that a separate character Mordwyd Tyllyon originally had no part in this story. He regarded the episode of throwing Gwern into the fire as in origin a test of whether the child was born of mortal parents or not. He suggested that Branwen was hated because she was a foreigner, and had been accused of being a fairy and consorting with demons. Had this been the case the fire would not have burned the child. As it is, he suggested, the child did burn, and thus got the nickname of Gwern Vorddwyd Tyllion, 'Gwern with-holes-in-his-thighs'. The extant version of the story, according to this explanation, is garbled because the redactor himself did not understand its significance, and felt impelled to patch it up (*Rhiannon* 63).

Mac Cana (162–5) advances good reasons for doubting this reconstruction of Gruffydd's. He refers to two lines from a Taliesin poem:

'*Bum y gan vran yn iwerdon
Gweleis pan ladwyt ymordwyt tyllon*',

suggesting the translation:

'I was with Brân in Ireland,
I saw when "the Pierced (Thick) Thigh" was slain (wounded)'.

He takes *y mordwyt tyllon* as referring to Brân, and compares (1) the wounding of Bendigeidfran in the foot and (2) the wounding of Chrétien de Troyes' Fisher King in the groin. The obscure saying in ll. 371–2 may be a quotation from a similar old poem and the poetic syntax of *Guern gwn* supports this suggestion. Gwern may just possibly have been 'the leader of the Irish who defended the cauldron which Brân had gone to take possession of'.

375. *peir dadeni*: see Introduction, pp. xxxii–iii. This cauldron of resurrection or regeneration (*dad-geni*) may also have the properties of a cornucopia. For the various properties of cauldrons see Loomis, *Wales and the Arthurian Legend*, 156–8.

379. *o wyr...*: logically, this follows on *calaned* (the corpses of the men ...).

383. *uonllwm*: mut. (after dual) of *bonllwm* 'bare-bottomed', i.e. breechless. See Mac Cana 116.

384. *Emystynnu idaw ynteu*: 'he for his part stretched himself'.

386. *o hynny*: 'because of that', i.e. because of the bursting of the cauldron.

y meint goruot a uu: 'such victory/survival as there was'. *goruot* (*gorfod*) may mean either 'victory' or 'survival' (= Lat. *superesse*) in the two contexts in ll. 386–7.

389. *Gliuieu Eil Taran*: 'G. son of Thunder'. *eil* here is an extension of *eil* (*ail*) 'second'; 'like', 'similar to'.

Pryderi: the only mention of him in this branch of the Mabinogi.

391. *llad*: (1) 'strike', (2) 'cut', 'sever', (3) 'kill'. The sense of (2) seems best in this context. I. W. compares the pagan Irish custom of

cutting off the head of a person slain in battle, and carrying it off as a trophy of victory. The comparison is not entirely happy.

395. *Adar Riannon*: they were three in number (see 427).

y canu: see l. 178 n.

395–6. *A'r penn a uyd kystal gennwch y gedymdeithas ac y bu oreu gennwch*: lit. 'and the head, its company (companionship) will be as good in your opinion as it was at best'.

397. *Guales*: perhaps Grassholm, an island off the coast of Pembrokeshire.

398. *Aber Henuelen*: probably the Bristol Channel.

398–9. *y tu ar Gernyw*: see l. 437 n.

400. *o'r pan*: 'from the time that'. Although *pan* does not seem to occur as a noun, this phrase is analogical with *o'r pryd, o'r amser*.

404. *Aber Alau*: the river Alaw flows into the sea slightly to the east of Holyhead in Anglesey.

407. *da a dwy ynys*: 'two good islands' (*a=o*).

409. *petrual*: 'four-sided', 'square'. The form in R, *pedryual* (*pedryfal*), is more regular, *pedry-* being the usual form in compounds. I. W. in a note on the word *tryfal* 'triangle' (*Bull.* xi 147) takes the second element to be the mut. of *mal*, which occurs in *cymal* 'joint', 'limb', 'branch'.

411. *y kerdet*: see l. 178 n.

414. *goresgyn o Gaswallawn uab Beli*, &c.: here, as elsewhere in Welsh tradition, Caswallawn (the first-century British hero Cassivellaunus) is said to be a son of Beli Mawr, who was regarded as an ancestor deity of the Welsh. There may well have been a separate saga concerning Caswallawn, a hero who was the son of a god, as suggested by Rachel Bromwich (SEBH 133). See also *Rhiannon* 75–76, 88.

417. *chwegwyr*: six men were killed, of the eight mentioned ('Cradawc and the seven men . . .'); Cradawc's heart broke; this leaves one survivor—Pendaran Dyfed (see 423).

418. *aniuyget*: *an-* neg.+*di-* privative pref.+*myged* 'respect'. The sense which fits the context best is perhaps 'bewilderment'.

420. *daroed*: used here as an auxiliary, much as in Mod. W. *daruot* (1) 'end', 'die', 'finish', (2) 'occur', 'happen' > auxiliary.

422. *geuynderw*: mut. of *keuynderw* '(male) first cousin' (*kefn* = 'conephew'+*derw* 'sure', 'true': Ir. *derb*). Cf. a similar use of Ir. *derb* in *derbbráthir*.

423. Both W and R here read *Pendarar*, not *Pendaran*.

429–30. *A fell dremynt oed udunt y guelet uch benn y weilgi allan*: 'and it was a far gaze (sight) for them to see them out over the deep'.

431. *ar hynny o ginyaw*: 'at that feasting'.

436–7. *y gayat*: see l. 178 n.

437. *y tu a Chernyw*: 'towards Cornwall', 'in the direction of Cornwall'. In ll. 398–9 W has *y tu ar Gernyw*. Cf. the two Gaelic idioms *taobh le* (= *tu a*) and *taobh na* (= *tu yr*). *tu ar* seems to combine both

NOTES

the usage with the prep. and that with the article. But I. W. takes *ar* as the old prep. meaning 'facing', which is more likely.

438. *ny dylywn ni y agori*: 'we have no right to (i.e. we should not, must not) open it'. With *dylyu* cf. Ir. *dligim*, *dliged*.

439. *yr a welsynt . . . yr a gewssynt*: the antecedent of the rel. *a* is in both cases implied in *a* and governed by *yr* (= *er* 'notwithstanding').

439–40. *yn y gwyd*: lit. 'in their presence', i.e. before their eyes.

440. *doy gof*: the reading of R, *doey y gof* '. . . the memory *of it*', is to be preferred.

444. *y uot yn hynny o amser*: lit. 'that it was that [much] of time', i.e. that it was so long a time. The text is not altogether convincing as it stands. *no* in l. 444 follows on *anesmwythach*, but not on the next clause. An interesting emendation is suggested in Loomis's *WAL* 150. We should perhaps read *y uot [yn hyn] yn hynny o amser* 'that he was older in (by) that time'. If this is accepted, the omission had presumably been made in the manuscript from which both W and R derive. G. and T. Jones (39) transl. this sentence, 'It was not more irksome than when they came there, nor could any tell by his fellow that it was so long a time'.

448. *yspydawt*: the meaning is uncertain. There is one ex. of a different form, *yspadawt* (479), which might be from *ysb* (pl. of *osb* 'guest') and *addawd* 'hall', 'dwelling'. Hence 'guest-hall', a concept common enough in the neighbouring Anglo-Saxon and Icelandic literatures. But this sense scarcely fits the contexts here. The senses of 'feast' or 'company', 'assembly' seem more appropriate. Perhaps 'festive assembly' may be suggested, but with misgivings. It may be a derivative in *-awt* from a borrowing of Lat. *(h)ospitium*. I. W. (*Bull.* vi 139) compares with *yspydawt* the form *yspeidawd*, which occurs in *Marwnad Cynddylan*, and suggests the sense 'company'. See also Mac Cana 144–5.

Loomis suggests (*WAL* 151) that *Yspydawt Urdaul Benn* and *Yspadawt Vran* are equivalent expressions, and that Brân himself was the *Urdaul Benn*, since *penn* meant both 'head' and 'chief'. Loomis goes on to surmise that the redactor of *Branwen*, taking *penn* in its physiological sense, decided that he 'had to concoct a preliminary story of Brân's decapitation and an appended tale of the disposal of Brân's head in the White Hill at London to accord with his misinterpretation'. Mac Cana (143) regards Loomis's theory as an oversimplification, but suggests that the redactor of *Branwen* may have used the pun on *penn* 'as a peg on which to hang his version of the "wondrous head" theme'.

Urdaul: many suggestions have been made as to the meaning of this word. The main ones are these:

   (1) that it stands for *uthrawl* 'wondrous' (i.e. referring to the head),
   (2) that it is an adj. from *urdd* in the sense of 'series', 'row'. If we

accept this, the word may be read so as to go with *ysbydawt*, with the sense of 'successive feasts' (but this would make the lenition in *Benn* hard to explain),

(3) that it is the mut. of *guirdaul*, an old spelling of *gwyrthiol* 'miraculous',

(4) that it is equivalent to *urddasol* 'honourable', 'noble'.

Mac Cana (141) compares the sub-titles in l. 448 and those in ll. 464–5 and 478–82, with the sub-titling of *Fled Bricrenn*.

449. *yd aethpwyt*: the interpretation of this phrase depends on that of *ysbydawt* (1) 'in which they went', (2) 'with which they went', (3) 'to which they went'.

450–1. *Meuyl ar uy maryf*: 'Shame on my beard'. I. W. suggests that the sense is 'shame on my manhood'. *bar(y)f* comes from Lat. *barba*.

453–4. *yd oed yn gyn hyspysset*: predicative *yn* is frequently omitted before an eq. adj., but its use is commoner before equatives beginning with *cy-*, or preceded by *cyn* as here (WS 52).

457. *gyuawr*: mut. of *kyfawr* 'moment', lit. 'beginning of an hour'; cf. *cyfddydd* 'beginning of day', *cyfnos* 'beginning of night'.

461. *matcud*: 'good or fortunate concealment'. The first element of this compound, *mat* (mad) 'good', survives mainly as a poetic word.

trydyd: 'one of three', not 'third'. There is a discussion of this triad by Rachel Bromwich in Loomis, *Arthurian Literature in the Middle Ages*, 45 ff.

462. *anuat datcud*: 'unfortunate disclosure' or 'exposure'.

ormes: mut. of *gormes* 'oppression', 'attack'.

463–5. *A hynny . . . yw hwnnw*: 'And that is what this tale tells. Their adventure is—"The men who set forth from Ireland"'.

These remarks round off the story of the journey from Ireland, ending with the burial of Brân's head in London and merely hinting at its later exhuming. This story within the story is given a separate title.

471. *lau heb lau*: the meaning is uncertain. I. W. suggested three possibilities:

(1) 'beside', 'by',
(2) 'with or without authority',
(3) 'promiscuously'.

lau (llaw) can mean 'authority', as well as 'hand'. *heb* can mean 'without', 'beyond', or 'past'. Although the sense 'side by side' would suit the context, it is difficult to reconcile with the usual senses of *heb*. I. W. prefers the sense 'promiscuously' (PKM 225).

473. *yll*: this is the prefixed pers. pron., 3 pl. It is used to reinforce a pers. pron. (or prep. pron.) before a numeral (WG 274; WS 73). See also l. 282 n.

474. *pymp rann*: 'the five parts' or 'divisions', referring to the five provinces of Ireland—Munster, Leinster, Connaught, Meath, and Ulster. The writer obviously knew of this ancient division, and his

NOTES

story of the five surviving Irish women is intended as an explanation of its origin. The story may well have been suggested by a native Irish tradition. See Introduction, p. xxxv.

475. The writer evidently was also aware of Irish treasures—golden and silver ornaments, &c.—and he concludes that these would have been discovered on battlefields. This is a good example of interpreting the history of one period in the light of another—the Irish grave-finds were more formally bestowed than the Welsh writer thought.

477. *geing*: mut. of *keing* f. 'branch', used here figuratively of a 'part' or 'section' of the Mabinogi. See *Math* 324.

478. *Paluawt Branwen*: 'blow (with the open palm) to (on) Branwen'. This is yet another reference to a previously existing triad—*Teir gwith baluawt ynys prydein . . .*—'the three unfortunate (left-handed) palm-blows of the island of Prydain'. According to the triad it was Matholwch who struck Branwen.

APPENDIX

FRAGMENT OF THE STORY OF *BRANWEN* CONTAINED IN PENIARTH 6, COLS. 52-54

This fragment corresponds to ll. 293-342 in our text

'... namyn a fo pēn bid bont. Mi a fydaf bont,' hep ef. Ac ena gyntaf y dywedpwyd y geir hwnnw, ac y diarhebir etwa ohonaw.

Ac ena gwedy gorwet ohonaw ef ar draws er afon, y byrywd clwydeu arnaw ef, ac yt aeth y lu ef drwod ar y draws ef. Ac ar henny, gyd ac y kyfodes ef, llema genadeu Mallolwch en dyfod attaw ef, ac en kyfarch gwell itaw, ac en y annerch y gan Uallolwch y gyfathrachwr, ac en menegi o'e uot ef na haethei namyn da arnaw ef. 'Ac y mae Mallolwch,' hep wy, 'en rodi brenninaeth Ywerdon y Wern uab Mallolwch, dy nei ditheu, uab dy chwaer, ac en y estynnu itaw y'th wyt di, en lle y cam a'r kodyant a wnaethpwyd y Uranwen. Ac en y lle y mynych ditheu, arglwyt, ae ema ae en Enys y Kedyrn, gossymdeitha Uallolwch.' 'Ie,' hep enteu Uendigeiduran, 'ony allaf i uy hun cael y urenhinaeth, oc oduyt ys kymeraf y gygor am awch kenadwri chwi. O hynn hyd hynny ny chewch chwi y gennyf i ateb eny del gennwch amgen noc a doeth.' 'Ie, arglwyt,' hep wy, 'er atep goreu a gaffom ninneu, ataty y down ac ef, ac aro ditheu en kennaduri ninheu.' 'Aroaf,' hep ef, 'o dowch en ehegyr.'

Y kennadeu a gerdassant racdunt ac ar Uallolwch y doethant. 'Arglwyt,' hep wy, 'kyweira atep a fo gwell ar Uendigeiduran. Ny warandawei dim o'r atep a aeth gennym ni attaw ef.' 'A wyr,' hep y Mallolwch, 'mae y kygor?' 'Nyd oes id gygor, arglwyt,' hep wy, 'namyn un. Ny ennis ef ymywn ty eiroed,' hep wy. 'Gwna di,' hep wy, 'o'e anrydet ef, ty y ganno ef a gwyr Enys y Kedyrn ar y neill stlys itaw, a thitheu a'th lu o'r parth arall. A dyro dy urenhinaeth en y ewyllis, a gwrhaa idaw. Ac o anrydet gwneuthur y ty,' hep we, 'peth ny gafas eiroed ty y gannei endaw, ef a dagnefeta a thi.' A'r kennadeu a doethant ar y gennadwri hono ar Uendigeiduran; ac enteu a gymyrth kymyrth. Sef a gafas en y gygor, kymryd henny; a thrwe gygor Branwen fu heny oll, a rac llygru y wlad oet genthi hitheu henny.

Y dagnefet a gyweirwd, a'r ty a adeilwyd en uawr ac en braff. Ac stryw a wnaeth y Gwydyl. Sef stryw a wnaethant, dodi gwanas o bop parth y bop colofyn o cant colofyn oet en y ty, a dodi boly croen ar bop un o'r gwanasseu, a gwr arfawc em hop un onadunt. Sef a wnaeth Efnyssyn dyfod ymlaen llu Enys y

APPENDIX 43

Kedyrn y mywn, ac edrych golygon arwyllt antrugarawc ar hid y ty a wnaeth. Ac arganfod y byly crwyn ar hyd y pyst. 'Beth yssyt yn y boly hwn?' hep ef wrth un o'r Gwytyl. 'Blawd, eneid,' hep ef. Sef a wnaeth enteu y deimlaw ef eny gafas y bēn, a gwasgu y bēn eny glyw y uysset yn ymanodi en y ureithell drwe yr asgwrn. Ac adaw hwnnw, a dodi y llaw ar un arall a gofyn, 'Beth yssyt ema?' 'Blawd,' medei y Gwydel. Sef a wnaei enteu er un gware a phawb onadunt, hyd nad edewis ef gwr byw o'r holl wyr o'r deu canwr eithyr un. A dyfod ar hwnnw, a gofyn, 'Beth yssyt ema?' 'Blawd, eneid,' hep y Gwydel. Sef a . . . .

(*Note*. Punctuation and paragraphing have been supplied for greater ease of comparison with the corresponding passage.)

VOCABULARY

THE arrangement of the Vocabulary *follows the roman alphabetical order strictly, with one exception*—words beginning in *ch-* are arranged separately after words beginning in *c-*. It should be noted that this results in several departures from standard Welsh practice. Thus, words with initial *c-* and initial *k-* are separated. It can readily be seen that this was the normal practice of the scribe of W, who prefers to write *k-* before the vowels *e, i,* and *y,* but *c-* before the vowels *a, o, u,* and *w*. He is not entirely consistent in this (cf. *kalaned* (376) and *karchar* (White Book Mabinogion, *passim*)), but the great weight of evidence in our text favours the above division. It may offend certain susceptibilities to find *u* = len. *b, f,* len. *m, u* all listed under *u*; or *f = f, ff,* and *ph* listed under *f,* but here I must plead that I had in mind the needs of students not familiar with the normal Welsh system. The forms in brackets give the pronunciation of words, using the values of the letters in Mod. Welsh. Mod. Welsh forms of certain words (if different from those of the text) are given, e.g. **aryant** (Mod. W. **arian**). A limited selection of Irish and Scottish Gaelic cognates is given for comparative purposes. Where there is a note on a word, n. appears after the line reference. Fairly exhaustive cross-references are given, as an aid to the student who is still finding his way in Welsh.

a 1. (len.) affirmative particle, used before the verb when preceded by the subjt. or obj. of the sentence, 1, 13, 27.

    2. (len.) subjt. or obj. rel. pron. (affirmative); used subjectively, 9, 16, 40; objectively, 33; with the antecedent **'r**, in the phrase **o'r a,** *of those that, of what,* &c., 112, 179 n., 356.

    3. (len.) interr. part., 33. See 261–2 n. See also **ae.**

    4. (len.) interj. *O!,* 122.

    5. (asp.) conj. *and* (before consonants), 2, 27, 29. See 30 n.

    6. (asp.) prep. *with,* 36, 81, 94. Used after eq. degree of adjs., 71, 98.

    7. equivalent to **o,** 407 n.

a'e 1. **a** 1.+**e** dep. gen. inf. pron. 3rd sg. or pl., 28, 121, 155, 419.

    2. **a** 6.+**e** poss. pron. 3rd sg. masc., 189.

    3. **a** 2.+**e** inf. pron. 3rd sg. or pl., 356.

a'r 1. **a** 5.+**(y)r,** *the,* 9, 58, 60.

    2. **a** 6.+**(y)r,** *the,* 17, 27, 77.

a'th, a 5.+**'th** inf. pron. 2nd sg., 319.

a'y 1. **a** 5.+**y,** *his, its,* 189, 235.

    2. **a** 6.+**y,** *his, its,* 114, 393.

VOCABULARY

3. **a** 1.+**'y**, q.v., 90. Cf. **a'e** 1.

Perhaps forms 1. and 2. should not be distinguished.

ac (ag) 1. conj. *and* (before vowels and **h-**), 2, 32, 37. See **a** 5.

   2. conj. *as* (used after eq. degree of adjs.), 83, 135, 396. Also **a** 6.

   3. prep. *with* (used before vowels), 7; used after eq. degree of adj., 114. See **a** 6.

achas, 479 v. See **achaws**.

achaws (Mod. W. **achos**) m. *cause, reason*, 91, 143, 380. In phrase **o achaws**, *because of*, 244, 259, 407–8; *concerning*, 477, 479.

adar pl. *birds*, 395, 482.

adaw. vn. *leave, leave behind, depart from, omit*, 87, 241, 338; past 3 sg. **edewis**, 340; past impers. **edewit**, 243, 416, 466.

adeilaw (Mod. W. **adeilio, adeiladu**) vn. *build*; past impers. **adeilwyt**, 327.

adnabot (adnabod) vn. *recognize, realize*, 234, 444.

aduyd (adfydd) *perhaps, it may be*, 307 n.

ae interr. part. (affirm.) containing copula, *is it?*, 70 v. Also **ay**.

ae ... ae disjunctive part., *either ... or*, 174, 206. Also **ay ... ay**, 305.

aerua (aerfa) f. *battle, slaughter* (O.Ir. **ár-mag** > Sc. G. **àrach**); pl. **aeruaeu (aerfaeu)**, 475.

aeth. See **mynet**.

aethant. See **mynet**.

af. See **mynet**.

agor, agori vn. *open*, 438, 452; pres. 1 sg. **agoraf**, 451; pres. subj. 2 pl. **agoroch**, 398, 400.

agoret (agored) adj. *open*, 436.

agos adj. *near*. In phrase **o agos**, *from near, at close quarters*, 20.

alar. See **galar**.

allaf. See **gallu**.

allan adv. *out*, 26, 189, 430; in phrase **o hynny allan(n)**, *thenceforth*, 146, 169, 172.

allyssant. See **gallu**.

am (len.) prep. *about, concerning; for; opposite*, 39, 63, 71; in phrase **y am**, *besides*, 6; **am ... pen(n)**, *around (my) head*, &c., *against (me)*, 173, 186. Prep. prons. based on **am**: 3 sg. m. **amdanaw**, 420; 3 pl. **amdanunt**, 18, 19, 175, and **ymdanunt**, 18 v., 19 v.

amdanaw, amdanunt. See **am**.

amgen, adj. *other, different*, 308 n.

amharch (Mod. W. **amarch**) m. *dishonour, disgrace*, 229, 273.

amlhau vn. *increase, multiply; spread*; pret. 3 sg. **amlawys**, 255.

amlyket eq. of **amlwg** adj. *plain, clear*, 430.

amranneu. See **amrant**.

amrant f. *eyelid* (Mid. Ir. **abra**); pl. **amranneu**, 75.

amryw adj. *diverse, various*, 347–9 n.

amser m. and f. *period, season*, 444; pl. **amseroyd (amseroedd)**, 210.

amylhawys, 255v. See **amlhau**.

anagneuedus (**an-** neg. pref.+**ta(n)gnefeddus**, *peaceful*) adj. *quarrelsome*, 65; **anhagneuedus** 65v.; **anygneuedus**, 108.

aner, anet. See **geni**.

anesmwyth adj. *uneasy, irksome*; compar. **anesmwythach**, 443, 445.

anfuruaw (**anffurfaw**) vn. *maim, disfigure*, 79.

anfuryf (**anffurf**) m. *disfigurement, maiming*, 76.

angassei. See **genni**.

anghynwys m. *lack of hospitality, refusal*; adj. *savage, fierce, loathsome*, 170 n.

anhebic (**annhebyg**) adj. *improbable, unimaginable*, 362.

aniuyget (**annifyged**) m. *unexpectedness, bewilderment*, 418 n., 423.

annerch m. and f. *greeting, salutation*, 299.

annyuyget, 418 v. See **aniuyget**.

anorles adj. *ugly, unsightly* (?); noun meaning *warrior, brigand* (?), 159–60 n.

anryded (Mod. W. **anrhydedd**) m. and f. *honour*, 318; **enryded**, 321; **anrydet**, 321v.

ansawd (**ansawdd**) f. *condition, state, quality*, 21.

antrugarawc (Mod. W. **anhrugarog**) adj. *merciless, ruthless*, 333.

anuat (**anfad**) adj. *bad, unfortunate*, 462, 478.

anuod (**anfodd**) m. *non-desire, unwillingness*; **o'm anuod**, *against my will*, 115; **oc eu hanuod**, *against their will*, 176–7.

anuon (**anfon**) vn. *send*, 230, 237; pres./fut. 1 sg. **anuonaf** 109; impv. 2 sg. **anuon,** 108.

anwyl (**annwyl**) adj. *dear, beloved*; **anwylet** eq., 83.

anwylet. See **anwyl**.

anygneuedus. See **anagneuedus**.

ar (len.) prep. *on, over*, 1, 28; *facing*, 393, 399; no mutation indicated, 50; used in expressing certain numerals, e.g. **teir llong ar dec**, *thirteen ships*, 13–14; **ar draws**, *across*, 297; **ar hynny**, *thereupon* (see **hwnnw**); **ar hyt**, *along, throughout*, 334; **ar ol**, *after*, 120; prep. prons. based on **ar**: 1 sg. **arnaf**, 73, 167, 396; 3 sg. m. **arnaw**, 160, 211 v., 297; 3 sg. f. **arnei**, 220, 229, 288; 1 pl. **arnam**, 163; 2 pl. **arnawch**, 162; 3 pl. **arnunt, arnynt**, 22, 31, 182.

arall pron. (also used adjectivally) *other*, 54, 84, 144; pl. **ereill**, 24. See also **neill**.

arbennic (**arbennig**) adj. *foremost, excellent, matchless*, 207.

ardiawc (**arddiog**) adj. *lifeless, listless*, 131 (**ar-** prefix with intens. force+**diawc**, *slothful, lazy*).

ardyrchawc (**ardderchog**) adj. *famous, conspicuous*; used with **o** in sense of *invested with*, 2 n.

arganuot (**arganfod**) vn. *perceive, catch sight of*, 333; past impers. **arganuuwyt** (**arganfuwyd**), 234.

arglwyd (**arglwydd**) m. *king, lord, master*, 31, 34, 36.

arglwydes (**arglwyddes**) f. *lady*, 270, 271.

arhoes. See **aros.**
arnaf, arnei, arnunt. See **ar.**
aros vn. *wait, await*, pres./fut. 1 sg. **arhoaf,** 311, **aroaf,** 311v.; impv. 2 sg. **aro,** 310; past 3 sg. **arhoes,** 187.
arouun (arofun) vn. *seek, make for*, 85 (**ar-**+**gofun**).
aruawc (arfawg) adj. *armed*, 166, 330.
aruchel (**ar-** intens. prefix) adj. *high, very high*, 266, 278.
arueu (arfeu), 196, 344, 371, *weapons, armour* (pl. of **aryf (arf)** f.) See the derivative adj. **aruawc.**
arwest f. *string (of musical instrument)*, 256 n.
arwreid (arwr-eidd) adj. *heroic, fine*, 22 n.
arwyd (arwydd) f. *sign, token,* 25; *banner, flag, pennon*; pl. **arwydon,** 22.
arwyllt. See **gorwyllt.**
aryant (Mod. W. **arian**) m. *silver, of silver,* 113, 475.
ascwrn (asgwrn) m. *bone*, 76, 337.
at, 224 n.
at (len.) prep. *to,* 78, 87; prep. prons. based on **at**: 1 sg. **at(t)af,** 161, 359; 2 sg. **attat,** 192, 310; 3 sg. m. **at(t)aw,** 40, 239, 299; 3 pl. **attunt,** 14, 16, 19.
ataw. See **at.**
atcassu (atgasu, ad- intens. prefix+**cas,** *hatred*) vn. *hate, loathe,* 170.
athrist adj. *very sad, grievous*, 133.
athrugar adj. *merciless, pitiless, cruel*; *huge, monstrous, loathsome*, 159 n.
atteb (Mod. W. **ateb**) m. *answer*, 40, 105, 106; **attep,** 309, 313, 314.
attunt (atynt). See **at.**
auon (afon) f. *river,* 254, 285, 286.
auorles, 160 v. Misreading for **anorles,** q.v.
auory (Mod. W. **yfory**) adv. *tomorrow*, 137, 140.
awch, 308v. See **ych.**
awr f. *hour*; **yr awr honn,** *at this hour, now*, 363.
ay, 70, 451. See **ae.**

badeu (Mod. W. **badau**), 26, *boats* (pl. of **bat (bad)** m.).
bali. See **pali.**
ban. See **pan.**
ban(n) f. *quarter, region, place* (Mid. Ir. **benn**), 196; **yn y uann,** *on the spot,* 195–6v.
barawt. See **parawt.**
barhawd. See **parhau.**
baryf (Mod. W. **barf**) f. *beard*, 450–1 n.
bed (bedd) m. *grave*, 409.
bei. See **bot.**
beichawc (beichawg) adj. *pregnant,* 467.

beichogi (i) *conceive, become pregnant,* 165, (ii) m. *pregnancy,* 209 (?).
beis (bais) m. (?) stepping, walking, wading 253 n., 277.
beth interr. *what?,* 32, 68, 94. Mut. of **peth**.
beunyd (beunydd) adv. *every day, daily,* 221.
bieu, 32 n. See **pieu**.
bit. See **bot**.
blawt (blawd) m. *meal, flour,* 335, 339, 342. See 347–9 n.
blwydyn (blwyddyn) f. *year,* 168, 208, 213; pl. **blwynyded (blwynyddedd**—more usually **blynyddoedd),** 226; pl. used after numerals, **blyned (blynedd),** 394, 398, 432.
blwynyded. See **blwydyn**.
bo. See **bot**.
bod (bodd) m. *(free) will; approval, permission,* 99, 176, 300.
boly m. *a (hide or leather) bag,* 330 n., 334, 347–9 n.; pl. **bolyeu,** 333, **byly,** 333v.
bon m. *bottom, base* (Mid. Ir. **bun**), 230.
bonclust m. *a box on the ear,* 220.
bonllwm adj. *bare-bottomed,* 383 n.
bont. See **bot**.
bore m. *morning* (cf. O.Ir. **imbárach**), 377.
bot (bod) vn. of vb. 'to be', 59, 87, 123; pres. 2 sg. **wyt,** 135; 3 sg. **yw,** 34, 35, 68; **mae,** 31 n. 69, 262, 292 n.; **oes,** 84, 107, 268; **yssyd (yssydd),** 30 n., 163, 286; **yssit,** 347–9 n.; 3 pl. **maent,** 194; consuet. pres. and fut. 1 sg. **bydaf (byddaf),** 294; 2 pl. **bydwch (byddwch),** 393, 397; 3 pl. **bydant (byddant),** 411; fut. 3 sg. **byd (bydd),** 141, 164, 166; imperf. 1 sg. **oedwn (oeddwn),** 156; 3 sg. **oed (oedd),** 1, 3, 28; 3 pl. **oedynt (oeddynt),** 13, 56, 245, 258; **ytoedynt (ydoeddynt),** 475; imperf. habitual 3 pl. **bydynt (byddynt),** 10, 38, 431; past 3 sg. **bu,** 42, 141, 145; 3 pl. **buant,** 168, 226, 432; past impers. **buwyt,** 41; pluperf. 3 sg. **buassei,** 446, 475; impv. 3 sg. **bit (bid),** 294; pres. subj. 1 sg. **bwyf,** 271; 2 sg. **bo,** 101, 113, 313; 3 pl. **bont,** 196v.; **bython** (corresp. to a 1 sg. form **bythwyf**), 196; imperf. subj. 3 sg. **bei,** 124, 199, 206; **pei,** 92 n.
brathu vn. *stab, wound,* 387.
brawt (brawd) m. *brother,* 5, 116, 228; pl. **brodyr,** 215; dual **broder,** 5 n., 368.
breichell, 337. See **breithell**.
breint (Mod. W. **braint**) f. *privilege, dignity, quality;* **ar ureint,** *after the fashion of, similar to,* 127.
breithell f. *brain, membrane of brain,* 337 v.
brenhin (Mod. W. **brenin**) m. *king,* 1, 17, 28.
brenhinaeth (Mod. W. **brenhiniaeth**) f. *kingship,* 302, 307, 320.
brenhineid (brenhinaidd) adj. *regal, kingly,* 434.
broder dual and pl. form of **brawd**.
bu, buant, buassei, buwyt. See **bot**.
bwrd (bwrdd) m. *board; deck; side of a ship,* 24.

VOCABULARY

bwrw vn. *throw, cast,* 140, 367, 383; past impers. **byrwyt,** 296, **byrywyt,** 296 v., 376; **bwrw allan,** *cast out, put out,* 26; **bwrw neit,** *make a leap,* 367.
bwyf. See **bot.**
bwyt m. *food,* 181, 426.
bwyta vn. *eat,* 128, 427.
by. See **pa.**
bychan adj. *small, little,* 113; **bychanet** eq. *how little,* 134, 136, **bychenet,** 136 v.
byd, bydant, bydynt. See **bot.**
bynnac (bynnag), *-soever;* **pa hyt bynnac,** *however long,* 458–9.
byr(y)wyt. See **bwrw.**
bys m. *finger,* 113; pl. **byssed (bysedd),** 337.
byt (byd) m. *world,* 441.
byth adv. *ever,* 462.
bythont. See **bot.**
byw adj. *alive,* 446, 466.

cad f. *battle,* 349 n.
cadarn adj. *strong, powerful;* pl. **kedeirn,** 38, 96; compar. **cadarnach,** 38 n.
cadarnhau vn. *strengthen,* 195.
cadbarawt comp. adj. *ready for the fray,* 349 n.
cadwedic verbal adj. *treasured, cherished,* 206 n.
cadwr m. *fighter, warrior;* pl. **kydwyr (kedwyr),** 349.
cae m. *clasp, brooch,* 206.
caei. See **caffael.**
cael. See **caffael.**
caffael, caffel, cael vn. *get, obtain; have, keep; reach, arrive at,* 124, 364, 368; pres. 2 sg. **kehy,** 136, **key,** 136v.; 3 sg. **geif** (mut. of **keif(f)**), 35, 111, 112; pres./fut. 2 pl. **keffwch,** 308, **kewch** (mut. to **chewch**), 308 v.; imperf. 2 sg. **caei,** 75, 132, 218; past 1 sg. **keueis (cefais),** 93, 168; 3 sg. **cauas, kavas (cafas),** 231, 322, 324; 3 pl. **causant (cawsant),** 178; past impers. **cahat,** 44, 241; pluperf. 3 sg. **cawssei,** 134, 214; 3 pl. **kewssynt,** 440; pres. subj. 3 sg. **caffo,** 150 n.; 1 pl. **caffom,** 309.
calaned (calanedd) pl. of **celain** f. *corpse, dead body,* 378, 382.
calon f. *heart,* 385, 408, 418.
cam m. *wrong, injury,* 134, 304.
cannwr, *a hundred men* **(cant+gwr),** 341.
cant, *a hundred,* 329.
canu vn. *sing, compose,* 345, 395, 428.
cany conj. [**can** (Mod. W. **gan**)+**ny,** neg.], *since . . . not,* 462.
canyat (caniad) m. and f. *singing,* 481.
canyat f. *permission, leave,* 72; also **ken(n)yat (ceniad),** 72v., 88v.; **canhyat,** 88.

car m. *kinsman; friend, companion*, 455.
carcharu vn. *imprison*; impv. 2 sg. **carchara**, 224.
caredic (caredig) adj. *kind, friendly*, 121.
carrec (carreg) f. *rock, stone*, 4, 29.
caru vn. *love*, 356.
cauas, causant. See **caffael**.
cayat adj. *closed*, 437.
cladu (claddu) vn. *bury*, 401, 409; past 3 pl. **cladyssant**, 460; impv. 2 pl. **cledwch**, 393.
clawr m. *plate*, 114 n.
cledwch. See **cladu**.
cledyf (cleddyf) m. *sword*, 419, 421.
clot (clod) m. and f. *fame, honour*, 209.
clotuawr (clodfawr) adj. *famous, celebrated*, 208.
clust f. *ear*; pl. **clusteu**, 74.
clwyd f. *hurdle* (Ir. **cliath**); pl. **clwydeu**, 297.
clybot (Mod. W. uses the alternative form **clywed**), vn. *hear, perceive*, 236 n., 273; pres. 3 sg. **clyw**, 337; imperf. 3 sg. **clywei**, 28, 344; pluperf. 3 pl. **clywssynt**, 428.
clyw, clywei, clywssynt. See **clybot**.
codyant (coddiant) m. *harm, hurt; disgrace; evil*, 304.
coet (coed) coll. *forest, trees*, 263, 266, 267.
cof m. *remembrance, recollection*, 440.
collet (colled) m. and f. *loss*, 454.
colli vn. *lose*; pluperf. 3 pl. **collyssynt**, 454, 455.
colouyn (colofyn) f. *column, pillar*, 329.
coron f. *crown*, 2.
coronawc adj. *crowned*, 1, 415.
corwg m. *coracle, skiff* (Ir. **curach**); pl. **corygeu**, 223 n.
corygeu. See **corwg**.
craf (craff) f. *grip, hold*, 75.
crib m. and f. *crest, top, ridge*, 180.
croyn m. *hide, pelt* (cf. O.Ir. **crocenn**), 330; pl. **crwyn**, 333.
crwyn. See **croyn**.
cud (cudd) m. *concealment*, 463.
cudiaw (cuddiaw) vn. *hide, conceal*; past impers. **cudywyt (cuddiwyd)**, 461.
cwbyl adj. *whole, complete, total*, 93, 145.
cwynaw vn. *complain* (cf. **coín-** in Ir. **coínim**, *I complain*), 239.

cheffwch. See **keffwch** sub **caffael**.
chenadeu. See **kennad**.
chenedyl. See **kenedyl**.
chenyt. See **gan**.
cherdet. See **kerdet**.
chwaer f. *sister* (Ir. **siúr**), 70, 71, 240.

VOCABULARY

chwedyl f. *tale, tidings, news* (Ir. **scél**), 78, 87; pl. **chwedleu**, 261, 262, 413.

chwegwyr, *six men*, 417.

chweiryaw, 126v. See **kyweiraw**.

chwi (O. Ir. **sí, sib**), pers. pron. 2 pl., 163; also as aux. aff. pron., 308, 316, 401.

chwythu vn. *blow*, 184.

chyhyt. See **kyhyt**.

chyuarch. See **kyuarch**.

chyuedach. See **kyuedach**.

chyweiraw. See **kyweiraw**.

da adj. *good*, 9, 37, 197, 407 n.; compar. **gwell**, 27, 59, 162; superl. **goreu**, 141, 196, 212; used as noun, *goods*; *good fortune*, 29.

dadeni vn. *regenerate, reanimate, renew*, 375 n.

dadleu m. *assembly, council*, 232.

dalo. See **talu**.

damunet (**damuned**) m. *desire*, 470. Also in the form **dymunet**.

damweinio vn. *happen*; past 3 sg. **damweinwys**, 209.

dan prep. *under*, 375; **y dan**, *up to*, 73.

dangos vn. *show, make obvious, declare*, 84 n.

danned. See **dant**.

dant m. *a tooth*; pl. **danned** (**dannedd**), 74 n.

darllen vn. *read*; past impers. **darllewyt**, 236.

darparu vn. *prepare*; also **darpar**, *preparation; intention*, 91.

daruot (**darfod**) vn. *finish, bring to a conclusion, die*; *happen*, 354; imperf. 3 sg. **daroed** (**daroedd**), 420 n.; past 3 sg. **daruu** (**darfu**), 415.

datcud (**datgudd**) m. *disclosure, exposure*, 462.

datcudiaw (Mod. W. **datguddio**), vn. *disclose, expose*; past impers. **datcudywyt**, 462.

daw. See **dyuot**.

dec (**deg**) num. *ten*, 14, 203, 239 n.

dechreu vn. *begin*, 52, 128, 130; past 3 sg. **dechrewis**, 375; 3 pl. **dechreus(s)ant**, 58, 62, 425, **dechreuassant**, 63 v., **dechreuyssant**, 128, 427; past impers. **dechreuwyt**, 183, 426, **dechreuit**, 183v.

decwlat, **degwlat**, 239 n., 480. See **gwlat** and note on l. 239.

deheu m. *right* (*-hand*), *south*, 14.

del. See **dyuot**.

delw f. *image*; **pa delw** (**pa ddelw**) interr. adv. *how*, 193 n.

deu (**dau**) num. adj. or noun m. *two*; governing nouns in the dual number, 5, 10, 280.

deuthant. See **dyuot**.

dewis m. *choice*, 174.

di aux. aff. pron. 2 sg., 271, 303.

diaerebir, 295v.

dial vn. *avenge*, 480; *vengeance, revenge*, 218.

dianc, diang vn. *escape, flee*, 387; past 3 sg. **dieghis, dienghis**, 190, 388, 424, **dihengis**, 190 v., 388 v. 3 pl. **dianghyssant**, 152, 153, **dihangyssant**, 153 v.

dianghyssant. See **dianc**.

diarhebir, 295v.

dieghis. See **dianc**.

diffeithaw vn. *lay waste, destroy*; past impers. **diffeithwyt**, 407.

diffeithwch m. *wilderness*, 467.

digrif adj. *pleasant, pleasing*, 439; compar. **digriuach (digrifach)**, 443.

digriuwch (digrifwch) m. *amusement, entertainment, pleasure*, 200.

diharebu vn. *utter a proverb, use as a proverb*; pres. impers. **diharebir**, 295 n.

diheu (Mod. W. **diau**) adj. *certain*, 20.

dilit (dilid, Mod. W. vn. **dilyn**), vn. *follow, continue*, 58, 197; **dilyt**, 60.

dilwgyr adj. *uncorrupted*, 399.

dim 1. pron. *anything, nothing*, 154, 264, 269.
2. adv. *(not) at all* (?), 440.

dioer interj. *God knows!*, 81, 92 n., 99.

diolwch (Mod. W. **diolch**) vn. *thank*; *thanks*, 141.

diruawr, dirwawr (dirfawr) adj. *very great*, 142, 188, 204.

disgynnu, diskynnu vn. *alight*; *decide*, 125, 233; past 3 pl. **diskynyssant**, 225.

diskynnat m. *one who descends on, an attacker*; pl. **diskynneit**, 348.

ditheu conjunctive indep. pers. pron. 2 sg., 303, 305, 310.

diuetha (difetha) vn. *destroy*, 117.

diuwyn (difwyn) adj. *unlovely, disagreeable, worthless*, 429.

diwall (**di-** + **gwall**, *defect, want*) adj. *abundant, lacking nothing*, 181, 439.

diwarauun (**di-** + **gwarafun**, *grudging, refusing*) adj. *without grudging*, 168.

diwed (diwedd) m. *end*, 201.

diwedyssei. See **dywedyt**.

dodi vn. *place, put*; *give*, 329, 330, 338; past 1 sg. **dodeis**, 175 n.; past impers. **dodet (doded)**, 146, 211, 244.

doet (doed). See **dyuot**.

doeth, doethant. See **dyuot**.

dof adj. *tame, trained*, 144.

doluryaw vn. *grieve*; *grieving, sorrowing*, 236.

doro. See **rodi**.

dothyw. See **dyuot**.

down. See **dyuot**.

dracheuyn, 224v. See **trachefyn**.

VOCABULARY

dremynt m. *sight*, 259 n., 429.
dricywys, 249v. See **trigaw**.
drwc (drwg) adj. *bad*; compar. **gwaeth**, 93; noun, *evil*, &c., 455.
drwod (mut. of **trwod (trwodd)**) adv. *through, across, to the other side*, 192, 273, 297; **drwad**, 273v.
drws m. *door*, 398, 400, 436.
drwy. See **trwy**.
drydwen (Mod. W. **drudwen**) f. *a starling*, 227 n.
drygweith m. *evil appearance*, 159 n.
dryll m. *piece, fragment*, 385.
dryllyaw vn. *break in pieces, cut*, 220.
duc. See **dwyn**.
duundeb (< **dy-undeb**) m. *unity, accord*, 352.
Duw m. *God*, 29, 137, 261.
dwy num. adj. or noun f. *two*, 185, 254, 280.
dwyn vn. *bring*; *spend* (of time); with **kyrch**, &c., *make*, 229 n., 442; pres. 1 sg. **dygaf**, 361; past 1 sg. **dugum**, 94; 3 sg. **duc (dug)**, 93, 208; impv. 2 pl. **dygwch**, 392.
dwyweith, *two times, twice*, 161.
dy (len.) dep. pron. 2 sg. *thy*, 70, 80, 85.
dybygy. See **tebygu**.
dydgueith (Mod. W. **dyddgwaith**) compound used as an adverb, *one day, on a certain day*, 65, 156, 233.
dyfynnu vn. *summon*, 179 v.; also **dyuyn (dyfyn)**, 179.
dygaf, dygwch. See **dwyn**.
dygyuor (dygyfor) m. *throng, host; gathering, uprising*, 41, 217.
dygyuor, dygyuoryaw vn. *rise up, muster*, 238, 282; past 3 sg. **dygyuores**, 172.
dylyedus adj. *due, proper*, 210.
dylyu vn. (i) *have a right to, deserve*, (ii) *be obliged to, have a duty to, owe*; pres. 1 pl. **dylywn**, 438 n.
dyn m. *man, anyone*, 365, 422, 466.
dyrchauael (dyrchafael) vn. *lifting, raising; prospering*, 24, 195.
dyro. See **rodi**.
dyscu (dysgu) vn. *teach*, 228.
dyuot (dyfod) vn. *come*, 14, 17, 33; pres. 3 sg. **daw**, 358; 1 pl. **down**, 310; 2 pl. **dowch**, 311; imperf. 1 sg. **down**, 92 n.; 3 sg. **doey, doy**, 204, 440, 462; past 3 sg. **doeth**, 37, 41, 78; 3 pl. **doethant, deuthant**, 50, 126, 126v., **doethan**, 445; perf. 3 sg. **dothyw**, 350; pluperf. **dothoed, dathoed**, 456, 456v.; impv. 3 sg. **doet**, 39, 117; pres. subj. 3 sg. **del**, 223, 308; in phrase **dyuot am penn**, *to fall upon*, 417.
dyuyn. See **dyfynnu**.
dywanu (followed by **y**, or more usually **ar**) vn. *happen upon, come on, find*, 66 n.
dywedassam. See **dywedyt**.

dywedut. See **dywedyt.**
dywedyt, dywedut vn. *say, speak of,* 78, 378; pres. 3 sg. **dyweit,** 464; past 3 sg. **dywot,** 371, 379; 1 pl. **dywedassam,** 65, **dywedyssam,** 252, past impers. **dywetpwyt,** 295; pluperf. 3 sg. **diwedyssei,** 106; pres. impers. **dywedir,** 452.

e 1. **(y)** def. art. *the,* 28 n., 78, 87.
    2. **(y)** (len.) prep. *to,* 449, 480; expressing purpose, 451.
    3. See sub **o'e.**
e gan. See **gan.**
ebol m. *colt, foal;* pl. **ebolyon,** 145, 146.
ebrwyd (ebrwydd) adj. *swift, fleet,* 15, 16, 311 v.; eq. **cyn ebrwydet,** *as soon (as), as quickly (as),* 352.
ederyn m. *a bird* (pl. **adar**), 227 n., 228, 230.
edewis, edewit. See **gadaw.**
edrych vn. *look, examine, see,* 18, 235, 279; past 3 sg. **edrychwys,** 453.
ef indep. pers. pron. 3 sg. m. *he, him,* 5, 29, 32; also aux. aff. pers. pron., 280.
ehegyr adj. *quick,* 311.
eidaw (Mod. W. **eiddo**) poss. pron. and adj. 3 sg. m. (used with def. art. **yr**), 35, 91. See also 18 n.
eidunt (eiddynt) poss. pron. and adj. *their;* **yr eidunt,** 18 n.
eighaw (ei(n)gaw) vn. *desire greedily, importune,* 171.
eil (Mod. W. **ail**) (i) ord. num. *second,* 147, 213, (ii) *son,* 389 n.
eill. See **gallu.**
eiryoet (eirioed) adv. *ever,* 21, 57, 263.
eissoes adv. *nevertheless,* 103.
eisted (eistedd) vn. *sit,* 3, 52, 128; past 3 pl. **eistedyssant,** 52, 129, 352.
eithyr conj. *except,* 141, 341, 378.
el. See **mynet.**
ell, 473v. See **yll.**
ellit, ellwch, ellynt. See **gallu.**
emystynnu (ymestynnu) vn. *stretch oneself,* 384.
en (yn) prep. *in,* 466.
eneit (Mod. W. **enaid**) m. *soul, life; friend,* 335 n., 342.
enghis. See **genni.**
englyn m. *englyn, stanza,* 346.
enni. See **genni.**
enryded. See **anryded.**
enryued (enryfedd < **an-** intens. part.+**ryfedd)** adj. *wonderful, strange,* 263v.
enw m. *name,* 211.
eny, 308–9v., 336v. See **yny.**
erbyn vn. *receive;* past 2 sg. **erbynneisti, erbynneist ti,** 193, 193 v.

VOCABULARY

erbyn prep. *by*, 140 n.
erchi vn. *ask, command* (foll. by **y (i)**), 36, 173; impv. 2 pl. **erchwch**, 17.
ereill (Mod. W. **eraill**). See **arall**.
eres adj. *strange, marvellous*, 82, 154, 264.
erwyd. See **herwyd**.
eskeir (esgair) f. *ridge*, 266, 267, 278 (Ir. **escir, eiscir**, *ridge, elevation*.)
eskyll (esgyll) pl. of **asgell** f. *wing*, 230.
estynnu, 303v. See **ystynnu**.
etwa(n) adv. *again, still*, 109, 474; **ettwa**, 474v.
eu dep. pers. pron. (in gen.) *their*, 15, 29, 63; **eu h-** before vowels, 15, 21, 176–7.
eur (Mod. W. **aur**) m. *gold*, 475.
ewch. See **mynet**.
ewyllus (Mod. W. **ewyllys**) f. *will, desire*, 320.
eyngassei. See **genni**.
eynt. See **mynet**.

fan (= **phan**). See **pan**.
fawb (= **phawb**). See **pawb**.
fell (= **phell**). See **pell**.
foen (= **phoen**). See **poen**.
ford (ffordd) f. *road, way*, 394, 459; used as adv. **ford (y)**, *where*, 475.
frynhawngueith. See **prynhawngueith**.
fy (nas.) dep. pers. pron. 1 sg. *my*, 72, 97, 104.

gadarnach. See **cadarn**.
gadu, gadael vn. *leave, let, permit*, 285–6 n.; fut. 1 pl. **gadwn**, 108; impv. 2 sg. **at**, 224 n.
gahat. See **caffael**.
galar m. *grief, sorrow*, 441.
gallu, vn. *be able*; pres. 1 sg. **gallaf**, 306; 3 sg. **eill**, 103, 287 n., 292; 2 pl. **gellwch**, 399, 400; imperf. 3 pl. **gellynt**, 72, 378; imperf. impers. **gellit (gellid)**, 77, 80, past 3 pl. **gallyssant**, 457.
galw vn. *call*, 354; pres. impers. **gelwir**, 473; past 3 sg. **gelwis**, 357; past impers. **gelwit**, 158, 254, 447.
gan (len.) prep. *with, in the eyes of*, 61, 69, 83; *by, on the part of*, 131; prep. prons. based on **gan**: 1 sg. **genhyf**, 82, 98, 117; 2 sg. **genhyt, gen(n)yt**, 37, 101, 102; 3 sg. m. **ganthaw**, 141; **gantaw**, 189, 216; 3 sg. f. **genthi, genti**, 47 v., 97, 47, 326; 1 pl. **genhym**, 262; 2 pl. **genhwch, gennwch**, 262, 308–9 v., 396; 3 pl. **ganthunt**, 15, 20, 124, **gantunt**, 403 v., **gantu**, 403. Compound prep. **y gan**, *from*, 149, 300, **e gan**, 356; prep. prons. based on **y gan**: 1 sg. **y genhyf**, 309; 1 pl. **y genhym**, 314–15; 2 pl. **y gennwch**, 262 v.

VOCABULARY

ganedigaeth (usually **genedigaeth**) f. *birth*, 407.
ganho. See **genni.**
ganthunt (Mod. W. **ganddynt**). See **gan.**
garrec. See **carrec.**
garwhau vn. *roughen, ruffle*, 233.
gauael (**gafael**) f. *grasp, grip*, 365.
gawssei. See **caffael.**
gehy. See **caffael.**
geif. See **caffael.**
geing. See **keing.**
geir (Mod. W. **gair**) m. *word, saying*, 295.
gelu. See **kelu.**
gelwit. See **galw.**
genhadeu, 109. See **kennad.**
genhyf, genhyt. See **gan.**
geni vn. *be brought forth, be born*; pres. subj. impers. **aner**, 165; past impers. **anet**, 210, 468.
genni vn. *find room in, be contained in*, 379; past 3 sg. **enghis**, 317, **eigwys, ennis**, 317 vv.; pluperf. 3 sg. **angassei**, 57 n., **eyngassei**, 57 v.; pres. subj. 3 sg. **ganho**, 318, **geingho, ganno**, 318 vv.; imperf. subj. 3 sg. **ganhei**, 322, **geinghei**, 322 v.
genti. See **gan.**
gerdet. See **kerdet.**
geueis. See **caffael.**
geuel (**gefel**) f. *tongs, pincers*, 180; **geueyl**, 180 v.
gewssynt, gey. See **caffael.**
glan(n) f. *brink, shore*, 258, 291, 409.
glo m. *charcoal, coal*, 181, 183.
glyw. See **clybot.**
glywys, 440 v.
godiwawd. See **godiwes.**
godiwes (**goddiwes**) vn. *overtake*; perf. 3 sg. **godiwawd** (**goddiwawdd**), 90, **gordiwedawd** (**gorddiweddawdd**), 90 v. (n.).
godwrw (**godwrf**, also **godwrdd**) m. *uproar, tumult*, 370.
gof m. *smith, blacksmith*, &c., 179.
gogof f. *cave*, 467.
gohir m. *delay*, 364.
golwg m. and f. *look, glance*; pl. **golygon**, 332 n.
gordiwedawd. See **godiwes.**
goreskyn (**goresgyn**) vn. *overrun, overflow*, 414; past 3 sg. **goreskynwys**, 255.
goreu. See **da.**
gorfowys (**gorffowys**) vn. *rest, repose*, 405, 458.
gormes m. *oppression, invasion*, 462.
goron. See **coron.**
gorssed (**gorsedd**) f. *mound, hill*, 157.

VOCABULARY

goruot (gorfod) m. (i) *victory*, (ii) *survival*, 386 n.
gorwed (gorwedd) vn. *lie, recline*, 296.
gorwyllt (< **gor-** intens. pref.+**gwyllt**, *wild*) adj. *fierce, furious*, 332 n.; **(g)arwyllt**, 332v.
gossed, 157v.
gossot (Mod. W. **gosod**) vn. *place*, 184; *make a pile*, 180.
gossymdeithaw vn. *maintain, make provision for*, 167 n.; impv. 2 sg. **gossymdeitha**, 305.
gouudyaw (Mod. W. **gofidio**) vn. *afflict, grieve*, 172.
gouut (Mod. W. **gofid**) m. *grief, affliction*, 439.
gouyn (gofyn) vn. *ask, inquire*, 66, 88, 338; past 3 sg. **gouynyssant**, 90; impv. 2 pl. **gouynnwch**, 270.
graf. See **craf**.
grayssaw (Mod. W. **croeso**) m. *welcome* (often foll. by **wrth**, *to*), 30.
grym m. *use* (the more usual sense is *strength*), 77.
guae (gwae) interj. *woe!, alas!*; **guae ui**, *woe is me!*, 380, 407.
guan (gwan) vn. *strike, push*, 73 n. (also **gwanu**).
guanas (gwanas) f. *hook, peg*, 329, 330; pl. **gwanasseu**, 330v.
guarauun (gwarafun) vn. *grudge, refuse*; past impers. **guarauunwyt**, 169.
guare (Mod. W. **chwarae, chware**) m. *trick, sport*, 103, 339.
guascu (gwasgu) vn. *press, squeeze*, 336, 344; pluperf. 3 sg. **guascassei**, 343.
guassanaethu (gwasanaethu) vn. *serve*, 181 n.
guedus (gweddus) adj. *seemly*, 22.
guefl (gwefl) f. *lip* (usually of an animal); pl. **guefleu**, 74.
gueisson. See **gwas**.
guell (gwell) compar. of **da**, *good*; idiom of, see **cyuarch**.
guenwynwaew (gwenwyn+gwaew) f. *poisoned spear*, 388.
guerendewis. See **gwarandaw**.
guyr. See **gwr**.
guyrda (gwyrda) pl. of **gwrda**.
gwaelawt (Mod. W. **gwaelod**) m. *bottom*, 287.
gwaered m. *descent, slope*; in phrase **y wayret (i waered)**, *down*, 20 n.
gwahard (gwahardd) m. *prohibition, embargo*, 222.
gwanu vn. *thrust*; past 3 sg. **gwant**, 365 n.
gwaradwyd (gwaradwydd) m. *insult, disgrace*, 93, 99, 101.
gwaradwydaw vn. *insult, disgrace*, 80, 82, 97.
gwarandaw vn. *hear, listen*; past 2 sg. **guerendewis, gwarandewis**, 121, 121 v.; imperf. subj. 3 sg. **gwarandawei**, 314.
gwaret (gwared) m. *deliverance*, 382.
gwarth m. *shame, reproach*, 132 v.
gwas m. *lad, servant* (Mid. Ir. **foss**), 9, 248, 423; pl. **gueisson**, 9, 63, 469.
gwastat (gwastad) adj. *level, smooth, constant*, 132.

gwchuiwch (= **gwchwywch**), *beware of*, 371–2 n.
gwedu (**gweddu**) vn. *become, suit, fit*; imperf. 3 sg. **gwedei**, 6.
gwedy conj. *after*, 20, 97, 178.
gweilgi f. *the sea*, 4 n., 253, 255.
gweisson. See **gwas**.
gwelet, guelet vn. *see*, 207, 418, 430; pres. 1 sg. **gwelaf**, 16; 2 sg. **gwely**, 84; imperf. 1 sg. **gwelwn**, 158; 3 sg. **guelei**, 356, 420; 1 pl. **gwelem**, 265; 2 pl. **gwelewch**, 264; 3 pl. **gwelynt**, 13, 24, 436; perf. 1 pl. (with **ry-**) **rywelsom**, 263; past 3 sg. **gwelas**, 196, 366, 378; 1 pl. **gwelsam**, 263; 3 pl. **gwelsant**, 59, 198, 259; past impers. **gwelat**, 274; pluperf. 3 pl. **gwelsynt**, 21, 439; impv. 2 sg. **weldy** (combined with pron., originally used as an interr.), 437; imperf. subj. 3 sg. **gwelei**, 406; imperf. impers. **gwelit**, 275.
gwernen f. *alder tree*; *mast of ship*; pl. **gwernenni**, 274 n., **gwerneneu**, 274 v.
gwir m. *truth*, 451.
gwiscaw (Mod. W. **gwisgo**) vn. *dress, dress for battle, arm*, 18, 420; past 3 sg. **gwiscawd**, 19.
gwlat (**gwlad**) f. *country, land, region*, 149, 171, 175 (Ir. **flaith**).
gwled (**gwledd**) f. *feast, banquet*, 52, 129, 200 (Ir. **fledh**).
gwledychu vn. *rule*, 472.
gwn, 372. See **ci**.
gwn. See **gwybod**.
gwna. See **gwneuthur**.
gwneit. See **gwneuthur**.
gwneuthur vn. *do, make, accomplish*, 47, 76, 81; frequently used, with vnn. of other verbs, as an aux., e.g. 27; pres./fut. 1 sg. **gwnaf**, 118, 363; 3 pl. **gwnant**, 68; imperf. 3 sg. **gwnai**, 339, **gwnaey, gwnaei**, 339vv.; past 3 sg. **gwnaeth**, 67, 86, 115, **(g)oruc**, 133 v.; 3 pl. **gwnaethont, -ant**, 27, 27v., 59, 64, **gorugant**, 62; past impers. **gwnaethpwyt**, 81, 100, 116; impv. 2 sg. **gwna**, 317; pres. subj. 2 sg. **gwnel(h)ych**, 84–85 n.; imperf. subj. 3 pl. **gwnelynt**, 123; imperf. impers. **gwneit** (**gwneid**), 98, 175; imperf. subj. impers. **gwnelit** (**gwnelid**), 99, 175 v.; pluperf. impers. **gwnathoedit**, 215.
gwr m. *man*, 65, 115, 134; pl. **guyr, gwyr**, 17, 19, 90. See **swydwr**.
gwra. See **gwrhau**.
gwraged. See **gwreic**.
gwrda m. lit. *goodman*. Used in sense of *leading man, noble*; pl. **guyrda** (**gwyrda**), 172, 284, 291.
gwreic (Mod. W. **gwraig**) f. *wife*, 152, 160, 161; pl. **gwraged** (**gwragedd**), 412, 468, 470; in compound **gwragedda** (= **gwragedd-da**), *gentlewomen*, 172.
gwres m. *heat*, 188.
gwrhau, *to do homage*; impv. 2 sg. **gwra**, 320.
gwrthot (**gwrthod**) vn. *refuse, reject*, 123.

VOCABULARY

gwybot vn. *know*, 224, 451; pres. 1 sg. **gwn(n)**, 149, 155, 272; 2 sg. **gwdost**, 291, **gwdosti** (gwdost+ti), 154; 3 sg. **gwyr**, 269; imperf. 3 sg. **gwydat**, 419; past 3 pl. **gwybuant**, 442; past impers. **gwybuwyt**, 182; pres. subj. 3 sg. **gwypo**, 269 n.; imperf. subj. 1 sg. **gwypwn**, 92.

gwyd (gwydd) m. *presence*, 303, 440.

gwydwic (gwydd-wig) f. *heap, cairn, funeral pile*, 380.

gwyn(n) adj. *white*; fem. **gwen(n)**, 153 n., 188.

gwynnyas adj. *white-hot* (< **gwyn(n)+ias**, *violent heat*), 153 v.

gwynt m. *wind*, 15.

gwypwn. See **gwybot**.

gwyr 1. See **gwybot**. 2. See **gwr**.

gwys f. *notice, summons; levy*, 239 (Ir. **fios**).

gwysc (gwysg) m. *track, trail*; **yn wysc y benn**, *headlong*, 365.

gyghor. See **kynghor**.

gymerth, gymerwn. See **kymryt**.

gyn. See **kyn**.

gyngytywys, 367v. See **kyngydiaw**.

gyntaf adv. *first* (mut. of **kyntaf**), 294.

gyr llaw (Mod. W. **gerllaw**) prep. *near (at hand), close by*, 266; **geir llaw**, 266 v.

gyrru vn. *drive*, 218.

gyscu. See **kyscu**.

gystal. See **kystal**.

gyt (gyd) in phrase **y gyt** *(all) together*, 38, 61v., 147; **(y) gyt a(c) (gyda(g))**, *together with, along with*, 5, 55, 112 (for **y** see sub **y** 4).; **gyt ac y**, *as soon as*, 298, 426–7 (emendation).

gyuedach. See **kyuedach**.

gyweirach. See **kyweirach**.

gyweirwd, 327v. See **kyweiraw**.

ha interj. *ah!*, 315v.

haearn. See **hayarn**.

haedu (haeddu) vn. *reach*; imperf. 3 sg. **haedei**, 301; **haedu ar**, *reach, happen to*, 301.

hanfod vn. *exist, be*; pres. subj. 2 sg. **henpych**, 261 n.

hansawd. See **ansawd**.

hanuod. See **anuod**.

hawd (hawdd) adj. *easy*, 117.

hayarn (Mod. W. **haearn**) m. *iron*, 152, 178, 188 (Ir. **iarn**).

heb defective verb, *said*, 16, 29, 31.

heb (len.) prep. *without*, 72, 88, 216, 471 n.

hediw (heddiw) adv. *today*, 140.

hela, hely vn. *hunt*, 156 (Ir. **selg**). See also 330 n.

heno adv. *tonight*, 135.

henpych. See **hanfod.**
herwyd (herwydd) prep. *because of, by*, 177 n., 364.
heuyt (hefyd) adv. *also, besides*, 138, 159.
hi indep. pers. pron. 3 sg. f., 206, 208, 275; used as aux., 429.
hir adj. *long*, 394 (Ir. **sír**).
hitheu conjunctive indep. pers. pron. 3 sg. f., 227, 229, 292.
hol. See **ol.**
holl adj. *all*, 282 n.; **hollwyr,** *all the men*, 340.
hon. See **hwnn.**
hun f. *sleep*, 60 (Ir. **súan**).
hun refl. pron.; **e (y) hun,** *himself*, 114, 119, 239; **dy hun,** 137 v.; **eu hun, e hun,** *themselves*, 170, 440; **ue (= fy) hun,** *myself*, 306.
hut (hud) m. *magic, enchantment*, 420.
hwnn demon. pron. or adj. indicating present place or time *this*; *this one*. The forms are: sg. m. **hwnn,** 334, 347, 464; f. **hon(n),** 2, 46, 96; neut. **hyn(n),** 225, 308; pl. **hyn(n),** 30, 68, 70.
hwnnw demon. pron. or adj. indicating distant place or time, *that*; *that one*. The forms are: sg. m. **hwnnw,** 10, 40, 73 v.; f. **honno,** 42, 45, 61; neut. **hynny,** 6, 40, 81; pl. **hynny,** 48, 90, 201 n.; in phrases, **ar hynny, yn hynny,** lit. *on that*, i.e. *then, thereupon*, 64, 73, 85, 202 n., **ar henny,** 298 v.; **o hynny,** *on that account, because of that*, 104, 386 n.; **yn hynny, ymysc hynny,** *in the meantime*, 207, 209, 226.
hwy compar. of **hir** adj. *long*, 199.
hwy. See **wy.**
hwyl f. *course, condition*, 208 (Ir. **seól**).
hwylbren m. *mast; yard-arm;* pl. **hwylbrenni,** 275 n.
hwylyaw vn. *sail*; past 3 pl. **hwylyssant, hwylyassant,** 252, 252v.
hy adj. *bold, audacious*, 17.
hyn. See **hwnn.**
hynny adv. *then, thereupon*, 202 n., 213, 215.
hynny. See **hwnnw.**
hyspys (Mod. W. **hysbys**) adj. *manifest, evident, palpable*; eq. **hyspysset,** 454.
hyt (hyd) prep. *to*; in phrases **hyt y(n),** *to, as far as*, 50, 64, 203; **hyd na(t),** *so that . . . not, to such an extent that . . . not*, 77, 79, 217; **hyt at,** *to*, e.g. **hyt attaw,** *to him*, 239; **hyt ban,** *until*, 308, 336, 469; **ar hyt,** *along, throughout*, 334, 369.
hyuryt (hyfryd < hy-, *easy*+**bryd,** *mind*) adj. *delectable, agreeable*; compar. **hyurydach,** 443.

i aux. aff. pers. pron. 1 sg., 72, 73, 94 v.
iach adj. *sound, whole*, 112.
iawn m. *right, satisfaction, compensation*, 124, 134, 136.

VOCABULARY

idaw, *to him*; sometimes used almost as a poss. adj. *his*, 3, 54, 91; *of his*, 232. Also **ydaw,** 115, 206. See sub **y** 2.
idi. See **y** 2.
ie, *yes*; *well!*, 39, 80, 103.
ieith (Mod. W. **iaith**) f. *language, speech*, 228.
ieuang adj. *young*, 424.
im. See **y** 2.
inheu conjunctive indep. pers. pron. 1 sg., 115, 167, 175.
it. See **y** 2.
iwrthi. See **y wrth** sub **wrth.**

kalaned, 376. See **calaned.**
kedeirn (Mod. W. **cedeirn, cedyrn**). See **cadarn.**
kedymdeith m. *friend, companion*, 455; pl. **kedymdeithon,** 209.
kedymdeithas f. *company, fellowship*, 396.
keimat m. and f. *champion, hero*; pl. **keimeit,** 348.
keing (Mod. W. **cainc**) f. *branch*, 477 n. (O.Ir. **géc**).
keissaw vn. *seek; try, endeavour*; pres. 1 sg. **cheissaf** (mut. of **keissaf**), 381.
kelu, vn. *conceal*, 216.
kenedyl (Mod. W. **cenedl**) f. *clan, kindred* (cf. O.Ir. **cenél**), 83.
kennad, cennad m. and f. *messenger*; pl. **ken(n)adeu,** 88, 89, 109.
kennadwri m. and f. *message, tidings*, 308, 310, 323.
kennedyf. See **kynnedyf.**
ken(n)yat. See **canyat.**
kerd (Mod. W. **cerdd**) f. *song, poetry, music; craft, art, occupation*, 198, 256, 428; **kerd arwest,** 256 n., *performers of instrumental music; minstrelsy.*
kerdet (Mod. W. **cerdded**) vn. *journey, go, move, sail*, &c., 410, 411; as noun, e.g. in sense of *motion*, 15, 162, 163; past 3 sg. **kerdwys,** 256; 3 pl. **kerdassant,** 312 v.; **ar gerdet,** *on the move, moving*, 266, 268.
keueis. See **caffael.**
keuyn (Mod. W. **cefn**) m. *back*, 75, 159, 257.
keuynderw (kefynderw) m. *first cousin (male)*, 422 n.
ki (Mod. W. **ci**) m. *a dog*; pl. **cwn,** 372.
kic (Mod. W. **cig**) m. *flesh, meat*, 220.
kilid, kilyd (kilydd) m. *fellow, companion*, 444, 472 (Ir. **céle**).
kilyaw (Mod. W. **cilio**) vn. *retreat*, 285; past 3 pl. **kylyssant,** 288.
kinyaw f. *feast*, 394, 431, 481.
kuodes, 298v.
kychwyn, kychwynnu vn. *rise, set out*, 48 v., 458v.; past 3 sg. **kychwyn(n)wys,** 201, 465; 3 pl. **kychwynassant, kychwynnyssant,** 48, 202, 402.
kyduot (Mod. W. **cydfod**) vn. *be with, dwell with*, 445.
kydwyr. See **cadwr.**

kyffes f. *confession*, 362.

kyflauan (kyflafan) f. *slaughter; injury; crime, outrage*, 362.

kyflet (kyfled) eq. adj. *as broad (as), equal in breadth (to)*, 114 n.

kyflym adj. *swift, quick*, 283.

kyfnot (Mod. W. **cyfnod**) m. *period, time*, 468.

kyfranc f. *adventure; story, tale*, 464.

kygyd (Mod. W. **cigydd**) m. *butcher*, 219.

kyhyt (Mod. W. **cyhyd**) eq. adj. *as long as*, 114.

kylch m. *circuit*; **yn eu kylch**, *around them*, 153; **yg kylch (yng nghylch)**, *around, round*, 184, 259.

kymeint (Mod. W. **cymaint**) eq. adj. *as great, as much*, 125v., 155.

kymell vn. *force*, 219.

kymryt (Mod. W. **cymryd**) vn. *take, have*, 44, 60, 125; pres./fut. 1 sg. **kymeraf**, 307; 1 pl. **kymerwn**, 39, 122; past 1 sg. **kymereis**, 167; 3 sg. **kymerth**, 142, 324; impers. **kymerwyt**, 283; impv. 2 pl. **kymerwch**, 391.

kymwt (kymwd, cwmwd) m. *commot*, 144 n., 146.

kymyscu vn. *mix, blend*, 183 (cf. Sc. G. **coimeasgadh**, *mixture*).

kyn (Mod. W. **cyn**) prep. *before*, 98, 169, 364 v.; **kyn no**, *before*, 132.

kyn conj. *although*; with neg. **kyn ny**, *although ... not*, 271, 359.

kyn, *as, so*, 83, 430, 454; **kyn ... a chyn**, *as ... as though*, 430-1; **kyn ... a chyt**, *as ... as though*, 454-6.

kynghanei. See **kynghenni**.

kynghenni vn. *find room in, be contained in*; imperf. 3 sg. **kynghanei**, 277.

kynghor (Mod. W. **cyngor**) m. *counsel, council*, 39 n., 44, 100.

kyngydiaw (cyn+cyd) vn. *intend, purpose, attempt, decide*; past 3 sg. **gyngytywys**, 367 v.

kynhelis. See **kynnal**.

kyniuer (kynifer), *as many, so many*, 454, 455.

kynnal vn. *support*; past 3 sg. **kynhelis**, 373.

kynnedyf (Mod. W. **cynneddf**) f. *peculiarity, magical quality*, 139, 291.

kynneu vn. *kindle*, 375; m. and f. *fire, blaze*, 366.

kynniuyat (kynnifiad) m. *warrior*; pl. **kynniuyeit**, 348.

kynsyniaw vn. *conspire, purpose*; past 3 sg. **kynsynwys**, 367.

kynt adv. *before*, 377.

kynueissat m. *principal officer, steward*, 249-50 n.; also **kynweisyat**, 250.

kyrchu vn. *make for, attack, charge*, 14, 85, 161; **kyrch** f. *journey; attack*, 93; past 3 sg. **kyrchawd (kyrchawdd)**, 355; **kyrchwys**, 188; 3 pl. **kyrchyssant**, 312, 425, 435; past impers. **kyrchwyt**, 144; impv. 2 pl. **kyrchwch**, 401.

kyscu (Mod. W. **cysgu**) vn. *sleep, celebrate nuptials*, 47, 60, 97; past 3 sg. **kyscwys**, 61, 69.

kystal eq. of **da**, *as good*, 71, 83, 98.

VOCABULARY

kyt (Mod. W. **cyd**) conj. *although, though*, 101; **a chyt**, *as though*, 456.

kyuanhedu (kyfanheddu) vn. *inhabit, dwell, people*, 472.

kyuanned (kyfannedd) m. *inhabited place, dwelling-place*, 235.

kyuarch (Mod. W. **cyfarch**) vn. *greet, address*, &c.; **kyuarch guell (gwell)**, *greet*, 27, 162, 299; **chyfuarch**, 162 v.

kyuaruot (Mod. W. **cyfarfod**) vn. *meet*, 412; imperf. subj. 3 sg. **kyuarffei**, 456.

kyuarwydyd (kyfarwyddyd) m. *story, tale*, 464.

kyuathrachwr (cyfathrachwr) m. *kinsman (by marriage)*, 300. See 36 n.

kyuawr (Mod. W. **cyfawr**) f. *moment, time*, 457 n.

kyuedach (cyfeddach) f. *carousal, the act of carousing*, 58, 60, 198.

kyueir (Mod. W. **cyfair**) f. *direction, place, spot*, 64 n.

kyuodi (Mod. W. **cyfodi**) vn. *rise (up)*, 62, 363; imperf. 3 pl. **kyuodyn(t)**, 377; past 3 sg. **kyuodes**, 298; impv. 2 pl. **kyuodwch**, 109.

kyuoeth (kyfoeth) m. *territory; people of a territory, subjects*, 173, 174, 194.

kyuoethawc (kyfoethawg) adj. *wealthy*, 476.

kyuref (kyfref) eq. adj. *as thick (as)* (< **cyf-**, *equally*+**rhef**, *thick*, Ir. **com-remor**), 113.

kyuuch. See **uchel**.

kyuurd(Mod. W. **cyf-urdd**) used as an eq. adj. *of such (high) rank*, 83 n.

kyuyng (kyfyng) adj. *narrow, strait, confined*, 177 n.

kyweirach compar. of **kyweir (cywair)**, *prepared, well-ordered, well-equipped*, 21 n.

kyweiraw vn. *prepare, set in order*, 126; impv. 2 sg. **kyweira**, 313; past impers. **kyweirwyt**, 327.

kyweirdeb m. *order, arrangement*, 127.

kyweithyd (kyweithydd) m. *troop, company*, 411.

kywilid (Mod. W. **cywilydd**) m. *shame, humiliation, dishonour*, 124.

lan. See **glan**.
lau. See **llaw**.
lidyawcaf. See **llidyawc**.
llad (lladd) vn. *strike; cut, cut off; kill*, 75, 117, 391 n.; imperf. 3 sg. **lladei**, 75v., 419; past 3 sg. **lladawd (lladdawdd)**, 345; past impers. **llas**, 402; pres. subj. impers. **llader**, 139.
llall, (*the*) *other*. See **neill**.
llathen f. *rod, staff* (in Mod. W. *yard*), 113.
llatheu, 113v. (n.).
llaw f. *hand*, 338; see **gyr llaw**; **lau heb lau** (i) *side by side*, (ii) *promiscuously*, 471 n.
llawen adj. *happy, joyful*, 41, 360, 361.
llawn adj. and adv. *full, fully*, 166, 376.
llawr m. *floor*, 187.

lle m. *place*, 105, 194, 195; also used adverbially, *where, whence* (with **o**), 28; in the phrases **yn y lle**, *immediately, forthwith*, 44; **yn lle**, *in requital of*, 303.

llei adj. *less* (compar. of **bychan**), 226.

llen f. *veil, mantle*, 420.

llessach compar. adj. *more beneficial, more profitable*, 198 n.

llestyr m. *vessel*, 287 (Ir. *lestar*).

llety m. *lodging, quarters*, 66.

llidyawc (Mod. W. **llidiog**) adj. *angry, wrathful*, 279; superl. **llidyawcaf**, 10.

lliwaw vn. *reproach, taunt*, 216 n.

llong f. *ship*, 13, 203, 277; pl. **llongeu**, 20, 21, 23, **llongheu**, 49, **llogeu**, 274v.

llonyd (**llonydd**) m. *calm, peace*, 217.

llu m. *host, army, faction*, 10, 297 v., 319; pl. **lluoed(d)**, 297.

llun m. *form, fashion*, 118.

lluossauc (**lluosawg**) adj. *numerous*, 195.

llwyr adj. *complete, entire*, 238.

llygat (**llygad**) m. *eye*, 280.

llygru vn. *damage, mar, spoil*, 79, 326; past impers. **llygrwyt**, 112.

llyma interj. *here is, here are, behold!*, 213 n., 298, 411.

llyn(n) m. and f. (i) *lake*, 157, 158, (ii) *liquid, drink*, 426 (O.Ir. **lind** > Mod. Ir. **linn**, *pool*, and **lionn**, *ale*).

llyna interj. *there is, that is, there are*, 163, 264, 477.

llynghes f. *fleet, ships*, 290 (Ir. **loingeas**).

llys m. and f. *court, residence of a king or chief*, 3, 18, 42.

llythyr m. *epistle, letter*, 229, 230, 234.

llyueryd (Mod. W. **lleferydd**) m. and f. *utterance, power of speech*, 141.

llywenyt 1. (= **llywenydd**) *happiness*, 142, 204.

    2. (=**llywenet**) eq. adj. *so happy*, 131–3 n.

lo. See **glo.**

longeu. See **llong.**

lu. See **llu.**

mab m. *son*, 1, 8, 53; pl. **meibon**, 7; pl. after num. **meib**, 469.

Mabinogi, Mabinyogi, 477v., 477.

mae. See **bot.**

mae, *where is?*, 292, 315.

maent. See **bot.**

maeth 1. m. *nourishment, fosterage*, 212.

    2. in gen. relationship *foster*, 215.

magu vn. *rear, nurse*; past 3 pl. **magyssant**, 469.

mal prep. *like, as*, 6, 128.

mal y(d) conj. *as, so that; how* (often in mut. form **ual y(d)**), 38, 52, 78; **mal nat**, *so that . . . not*, 223.

VOCABULARY

mam f. *mother*, 5, 116, 472; **brawt un uam**, *a uterine brother*, 116.
maraf, 451 v. See **baryf**.
march m. *horse*, 111; pl. **meirych, meirch**, 63, 66, 70.
marchawc (marchawg) m. *horseman, mounted man*, 243, 244.
maryf nas. mut. of **baryf**.
matcud (matgudd) m. *good or fortunate concealment*, 461 n.
mawr adj. *big, great, much*, 42, 158, 159; compar. **mwy**, 72, 102, 124; superl. **mwy(h)af**, 11, 370.
may, mae (Mod. W. **mai**) conj. *that it is*, 116.
med (medd) defective verb, *says*; imperf. 3 sg. **medei**, 339.
medu (meddu) vn. *possess, own*; imperf. 3 sg. **medei**, 100.
medwi (meddwi) vn. *become drunk*, 183.
medwl (meddwl) m. *thought, mind*, 362.
medylyaw (meddyliaw) vn. *think, intend*, 133; past 3 pl. **medylyssant**, 123, 470, **medylyassant**, 123 v.
megin f. *bellows*, 185; pl. **megineu**, 184, 185.
meib, meibon. See **mab**.
meichiad m. *swineherd*; pl. **meicheit**, 258 n.
mein (Mod. W. **main**) pl. of **maen** m. *stone*, 286.
meint m. *quantity*, 386 n.
meirch, meirych. See **march**.
meithryn, vn. *nourish, rear*, 227, 234.
melyngoch compound adj. *reddish yellow* (of hair), 158.
menegi vn. *tell, relate*, 106, 228, 300; pres./fut. 1 sg. **managaf**, 156; past 3 pl. **managyssant**, 120; impv. 2 pl. **menegwch**, 111, 114.
merch f. *daughter, girl*, 8, 37, 95.
meuyl (mefyl) m. *disgrace, shame*, 381, 450.
mi indep. pers. pron. 1 sg. *I*, 16, 94, 103.
minheu conjunctive indep. pers. pron. 1 sg., 40, 72, 193.
mi(s) m. *month*, 164, 166, 170.
miui (Mod. W. **myfi**) indep. pers. pron. (doubled) 1 sg., 294 v.
mlyned (mlynedd). See **blwydyn**.
moch pl. *swine, pigs*, 259.
modrwy f. *ring*, 206.
mor m. *sea*, 64, 274, 463.
morben m. *coast, coastal district*; *headland*; pl. **morbennyd(d)**, 283.
morwyn f. *maiden, virgin*, 46, 71, 82.
mot, 380, nas. mut. of **bot**.
mwrthwl m. *hammer*, 180; pl. **myrthwl**, 180 v.
mwyaf. See **mawr**.
mwynant, 79 v. See **mwynyant**.
mwynyant m. *use, value*; *enjoyment*, 79.
mynet (myned) vn. *go*, 18, 91, 107; pres./fut. 1 sg. **af**, 40; imperf. 3 pl. **eynt**, 176; past 3 sg. **aeth**, 40, 89, 122; 3 pl. **aethant**, 60, 120, 199; past impers. **aethpwyt**, 449; impv. 3 sg. **aet**, 360; 2 pl. **ewch**, 111; pres. subj. 3 sg. **el**, 223; 3 pl. **elont**, 224 v.

mynnu vn. *desire, wish*, 35, 137; pres. 3 sg. **myn(n)**, 32–33 n., 37; imperf. 3 sg. **mynnei**, 421 v., **mynhei**, 421; pres. subj. impers. **mynhir**, 81; pres. subj. 2 sg. **mynnych**, 305; 3 sg. **mynho, mynno,** 119, 119 v.; imperf. subj. 3 sg. **myn(n)hei**, 32–33 n.; 3 pl. **mynhynt,** 82.

mynyd (mynydd) m. *mountain*, 265, 267, 275; **y uynyd** adv. *up*, 20 n., 25, 363–4.

mywn. See **ymywn.**

na (len.) neg., 21, 33, 141.

na conj. *nor*, 100, 205; **na . . . na,** *neither . . . nor*, 117, 287.

nac neg. (before initial vowel), 413; **nac . . . nac,** *neither . . . nor*, 441.

nachaf interj. *behold!*, 23 n., 65, 131.

namyn conj. *but, except, only*, 56, 85, 190.

nat (nad) rel. form of neg. *that . . . not*, 98, 117. See also sub **hyt.**

neb pron. *anybody*, (preceded or foll. by neg. *nobody*), 93, 190, 196; with the art., **y neb,** *the one*, 99; **na neb,** *nor anyone*, 100.

neges f. *errand, message,* 34, 35.

negessawl adj. *engaged on an errand*, 34.

nei m. *nephew,* 302, 359, 422 (Ir. **nia**).

neill (Mod. W. **naill**), *the one* (implying contrast with **y llall,** *the other*). The usual form in Mod. W. is **y naill . . . y llall,** cf. 9–11; commoner in this text, **neill . . . arall,** 54, 319–20, 351–2.

neit (Mod. W. **naid**) f. *leap*, 367.

nessaf superl. of **agos,** *near*, 216.

nessau vn. *approach, come nearer*, 16, 27; past 3 sg. **nessawys,** 25; 3 pl. **nessayssant,** 19.

neuad, 127 v. See **yneuad.**

ni indep. pers. pron. 1 pl., *we*, 122.

ni aux. aff. pers. pron. 1 pl., 66 v., 163, 252.

ni. See **ny.**

ninheu conjunctive indep. pers. pron. 1 pl., 39, 310, 311.

nit. See **nyt.**

niuer, 50, 62, 252 v. See **yniuer.**

niuyget, 423 v. See **aniuyget.**

niwaradwydaw nas. mut. of **di-waradwydaw** vn. *free from disgrace, take away disgrace,* 104. See **gwaradwydaw.**

niwed nas. mut. of **diwed.**

no, noc (asp.) conj. *than* (**noc** used before initial vowel); introduces the second element of the comparison, after compar. grade of adj., 21, 60, 124.

noe f. *shallow vessel; kneading-trough,* 227. (Mid. Ir. **nó (noe),** a (small) boat).

nos f. *night,* 42, 135, 147.

ny (Mod. W. **ni**) (asp., len.) indep. neg., 56, 72, 92, 108.

ny (< **yn y**), *where,* 75 n.

VOCABULARY

nys (**ny** neg.+**'s** inf. pron. 3 sg.), 108 n.
nyt (Mod. W. **nid**) indep. neg., 56, 84, 99 (used before vowels).

o, oc (len.) prep. *from, of, on the part of* (**oc** occurs before pl. gen. pronouns), 2, 20, 62; 176, 428; prep. prons. based on **o**: 3 sg. m. **ohonaw**, 295, 296; f. **oheni**, 405; 3 pl. **ohonunt**, 80, 331, 340, **onadunt**, 331 v., 340 v.
o'e (len.), **o** prep. *from*+**e (y)** inf. dep. pers. pron. 3 sg. m., 8.
o'm, o prep. *of*+**'m** inf. pron. 1 sg., 115, 191.
o'r, o prep. *of, from*+**yr**, *the*, 9, 23, 28; in sense of *on the*, 54. See also **a 2**.
o'y 1. **o** prep. *of, from*+**y** 3., 176; **oe**, 176v.
    2. *to his, in his*, 318 n.
och interj. *O!, alas!*, 275.
oduyt, 307v. See **aduyd**.
odyno (oddyno), *thence*, 47, 154, 190 v.; **odyna**, 144, 190.
oed m. *time, appointment, tryst*, 47.
oed (oedd), oedwn, oedynt. See **bot**.
oes. See **bot**.
of. See **gof**.
ohir. See **gohir**.
ol m. *rear, track*, 15; **ar ol**, *after*, 120; **yn ol**, *after*, **yn y ol**, &c., *after him*, &c., 160, 189.
oll adj., also used as pron. or adv., *all, completely*, 178, 326; sometimes reinforcing **pob**, e.g. **pob peth oll**, *everything*, 268.
onadunt. See **o**.
ony conj.+neg. *if not, unless*, 154, 217, 306.
onys (**ony**, *unless*+**s** inf. pron. 3 sg.), 269.
onyt (onid) neg. conj. *if not, unless*, 34, 413, 451.
oreskynwys. See **goreskyn**.
oreu mut. of **goreu**. See **da**.
orfowys. See **gorfowys**.
ormes. See **gormes**.
oruc. See **gwneuthur**.
orugant. See **gwneuthur**.
orwyllt. See **gorwyllt**.
os (**o** conj.+3 sg. pres. of copula), *if it is*, 37, 82, 123.
ot (od) conj. *if*, 160.
ouut. See **gouut**.
ouyn, ouynyssant. See **gouyn**.
oy interj. *alas!*, 380, 406.
oydynt var. spelling of **oedynt**. See **bot**.

pa (len.) interr. adj., *what*, 18, 91, 115; as substantive, 415; **py**, 35.
paham, interr. *why?*, 358.
pali m. *satin, brocaded silk*, 22 n.

pall m. *tent, pavilion*; pl. **palleu**, 56 n., 127.
paluawt (palfawd) f. *a blow with the open palm* **(palf)**, 478 n., 480.
pan conj. and interr. *when, whence*, 59, 148, 198; **ban**, 10.
pan yw, *that it is*, 115.
par. See **peri**.
parawt (Mod. W. **parod**) adj. *ready*, 178.
parei. See **peri**.
parhau vn. *last, endure*; past 3 sg. **parhawd (parhawdd)**, 144, **parhaawd**, 144 v.
parth m. *part, side*, 54, 267, 278; in the compound prep. **parth a(c)**, *towards*, 14, 17, 27. See 290–1 n.
pawb pron. *each one, every one, all*, 369, 370; **pawb o**, *all (of)*, 62, 340, 356; **pob** pronom. adj. *each, every*, 64, 112, 185.
pebyll m. *tent, pavilion*; pl. **pebylleu**, 126 n.
pedeir num. adj. or noun f. *four*, 239, 480.
pedwar num. adj. or noun m. *four*, 385.
pedwarugeint, *four score, eighty*, 397, 441, 447.
pedwyryd (pedwyrydd) ord. num. m. *fourth*, 169.
pei conj. *if*, 92 n.
peir (Mod. W. **pair**) m. *cauldron*, 139, 140, 148 (Ir. **coire**).
pell adj. *distant*, 429.
pen(n) m. *head, end, top*, 4, 29, 156; pl. **penneu**, 74, 343; **ym pen(n)**, *at the end of; for*, 164, 373 (cf. Sc. G. **an ceann**); **ar benn**, *at the end of*, 165; see **uchel**.
pennaf (also **penhaf**) superl. of **penn**, *head*.
   (1) adj. *chief*, 242, 250.
   (2) adv. **yn benhaf (oll)**, *especially, above all*, 457.
   (3) m., *chief, leader*, 31.
perchen m. *owner, possessor*, 180.
peri vn. *cause*, 170, 180, 181; imperf. 3 sg. **parei**, 9, 11 : past 3 sg. **peris**, 238, 391; impv. 2 sg. **par**, 222.
perued (perfedd) m. *middle*, 187 v.
peth m. *thing*, 268; in sense of *because*, 321–2 n.
pethewnos (Mod. W. **pythefnos, pythewnos**) f. *fortnight*, 164 n., 166.
petrual adj. *four-sided, square*, 409 n.; **pedryual**, 409 v.
phan. See *pan*.
pieu, *whose is?, who owns?*, 30 n., 32; **pioed (pioedd)**, *whose was (were)?*, 67.
plant m. *children*, 182.
pleit (Mod. W. **plaid**) f. *side-wall, partition*, 188, 189.
pluf pl. *plumage, feathers*, 233.
pob. See **pawb**.
pobi vn. *bake*, 219 (Ir. **cóc(aire)** (?)).
poen f. *punishment, penance*, 221, 236, 240; pl. **poeneu**, 229.
poethi vn. *heat, be heated, burn*; **poeth**, 366.
pont f. *bridge*, 289, 293, 294.

VOCABULARY

post m. *post, pillar*; pl. **pyst**, 334.
praf (praff) adj. *large, extensive*, 328.
prenn m. *tree*, 264 (Ir. **crand, crann**).
prif adj. *chief*, 46, 96.
prynhawngueith, *one afternoon*, 2 n.
pum(p), pym(p) num. adj. *five*, 466, 468, 469, 473.
purwen adj. *pure white, white-hot*, 186.
pwy interr. pron. *who?*, 30, 150, 419.
pym(p). See **pum(p)**.
pyst. See **post**.

'r. See **yr** 2.
rac (Mod. W. **rhag**) prep. *before, against; because of; lest*, 23, 188, 224; prep. prons. based on **rac**: 2 pl. **racoch**, 401; 3 pl. **racdu**, 312 n., **racdunt**, 312 v.
racco adv. *yonder*, 16, 437.
raculaenu (Mod. W. **rhagflaenu**) vn. *precede, outstrip*, 23.
rann (Mod. W. **rhan**) f. *part, share, division*, 474 n.
rannu vn. *divide, apportion; quarter*, 64, 194, 472.
ran(n)yat (Mod. W. **rhaniad**) m. *division, billeting, quartering*, 63, 473.
rawn (Mod. W. **rhawn**) coll. *coarse hair, horse-hair*, 75 n.
rei (Mod. W. **rhai**) pron. *some, ones*; commonly used with art. and (demonstrative) adj., 23; **y rei hyn(n)**, *these*, 68, 70; **a'r rei**, *and these*, 216 v.; **y rei ereill**, *the others*, 344.
reit (Mod. W. **rhaid**) m. *need, necessity* (foll. by **y (i)** 2.), *need for (to)*, 176.
reuedawt (rhyfeddawd) m. *marvel, strange thing*, 94.
rieni, *ancestors*, 45–46 n., 96.
rith (Mod. W. **rhith**) m. *form, guise*, 383 (Ir. **richt**).
rodes, rodho, rodi, rodo, rodyssant. See **rodi**.
rodi (**rhoddi**, Mod. W. **rhoi**) vn. *give*, 45, 72, 82; pres./fut. 1 sg. **rodaf**, 139; imperf. 3 sg. **rodei**, 206; past 2 sg. **rodeist**, 148; 3 sg. **roes**, 193, **rodes**, 193 v.; 3 pl. **rodyssant**, 83; pluperf. 3 sg. **rodassei**, 106 v.; impv. 2 sg. **doro**, 320 n., **dyro**, 320 v.; pres. subj. 3 sg. **rodo**, 29, 261, **rodho**, 29 v.
roes. See **rodi**.
rot. See **rwng**.
rugyl (Mod. W. **rhugl**) adj. *free, ready*; (used of ships' motion), 15.
rwg. See **rwng**.
rwng (Mod. W. **rhwng**) prep. *between*, 368, 373; often in the form **y rwng**, 42 or **y rwg**, 10; prep. prons. based on **(y) rwng**: 2 sg. **y rot** (Mod. W. **rhyngot**), 286; 3 pl. **ryngtunt** (Mod. W. **rhyngddynt**), 353 v., 473 v., **rydunt**, 353, 473.
rwymaw (rhwymaw) vn. *bind, tie*; past impers. **rwymwyt**, 230.
rydunt. See **rwng**.
rygynneryw, 94 v. See 94 n.
rygyueryw, **ry-** perf. part. + **kyueryw** perf. 3 sg. of **kyuaruot** *meet*,

happen to (foll. by **a** prep. *with*), 94 n.
rym. See **grym.**
ryued (Mod. W. **rhyfedd**) adj. *strange, marvellous*, 97, 263.
ryw (Mod. W. **rhyw**) indef. pron. used adjectivally and substantivally, *kind of, sort of*, 35, 115, 163 v.

sarahet, sarhaet (Mod. W. **sarhad**) m. *insult, act of violation, wrong*, 218, 218 v.; pl. **sarahedeu, sarhaedeu,** 171 n., 171 v.
sef (< **ys**+**ef**), *he is, this is, that is* (*to say*), *namely*, 10 n., 44, 52.
seith num. adj. *seven*, 243, 244; as substantive, 249.
seithuet (seithfed) ord. num. *seventh*, 433.
seithugeint, *seven score, one hundred and forty*, 239, 480.
seithwyr, *seven men*, 242, 245, 388.
somm f. (?) *trick, shameful trick*, 214 n.
stlys, 319v. See **ystlys.**
stryw, 328v. See **ystryw.**
sugyn m. *suction*; **mein sugyn,** 286-7 n.
swch f. *point*, 25 n.
swydwr (swydd-wr) m. *official*; pl. **swydwyr,** 62.
synyaw vn. *attend to, look after*, 249.

tal f. *payment, tally*, 145.
tal m. *front, end*, 227.
talu vn. *pay, hand over* (*in payment*), 137; pres. subj. 3 sg. **talo,** 138; past impers. **talwyt,** 143, 145.
tan m. *fire*, 183, 366, 367.
tangneued (tangnefedd) f. *peace*, 9, 25, 118.
tangneuedu vn. *make peace*; pres. 3 sg. **tangnoueda,** 322, **tangneuedha, dagnefeta,** 322 vv.
tangneuedus adj. *peaceful*, 126.
taraw (Mod. W. **taro**) vn. *strike*, 189, 220.
taryan (tarian) f. *shield*, 24, 374, **tarean,** 369.
tebyg adv. *likely*; compar. **tebygach,** 124.
tebygu vn. *think, suppose*; *supposing*, e.g. **o'm tebygu,** lit. *of my supposing, I suppose*, 191; pres. 1 sg. **tebygaf,** 103; 2 sg. **dybygy (dy- = de-),** 271.
tec, teg (teg) adj. *fair*, 22, 434; superl. **teccaf,** 46.
teimlaw vn. *feel, handle*, 336, 343.
teir num. adj. or noun f. *three*, 13, 203, 226; **teir . . . ar dec,** *thirteen*.
telediw adj. *handsome, fair*, 208.
telediwaw vn. *enhance, augment*; pres./fut. 1 sg. **telediwaf,** 138 n.
teruynu (terfynu) vn. *end, finish*; pres. 3 sg. **teruyna,** 477.
teulu m. *retinue, household*, 10 v.
teyrnas f. *kingdom*; pl. **tyrnassoed(d),** 256.
teyrndlws m. *royal jewel*, 206.
ti indep. pers. pron. 2 sg. *thou*, 81; also as aux. pers. pron., 34, 37, 310.

VOCABULARY

tidy indep. pers. pron. (doubled) 2 sg. *thou*, 36.
tir m. *land*, 17, 27, 33.
tiryon adj. *friendly, courteous*, 358.
titheu. See **ditheu.**
torllwyth m. *foetus, pregnancy*, 165 (**tor**, *belly*+**llwyth**, *load*).
torri vn. *break, cut*, 73, 286, 408; pres. 3 sg. **tyrr**, 384; past 3 sg., **torres**, 423; 3 pl. **torryssant**, 288.
tra conj. *while, as long as*, 197, 463.
trachefyn (Mod. W. **trachefn**) adv. *again*, 224.
traet. See **troet.**
tran(n)oeth lit. *over (beyond) the night*, i.e. *on the morrow*, 44, 61, 143; also **drannoeth**, 377 v.
traws m. *traverse*; **ar traws** prep. *across*, 296, 297, **ar draws**, 296 v.
tref f. *homestead, hamlet*, 244.
tremic (tremyg) m. *insult*, 72, 102.
treulaw vn. *spend, pass*, 210; past 3 pl. **treulyssant**, 200, 441.
tri num. adj. or noun m. *three*, 427.
trigaw vn. *stay, dwell*; past 3 sg. **trigwys**, 249, **tricywys**, 249 v.
trin f. *battle*, 348.
trist adj. *sad, sorrowful*, 132.
troet (troed) m. *foot*, 388; pl. **traet (traed)**, 364.
troi vn. *turn; walk about, be busied with*, 259.
trwy (also mut. form **drwy**) prep. *through, in, by*, 200, 285, 288; prep. pron. based on **trwy**: 3 sg. f. **drwydi (drwyddi)**, 292.
trwyn m. *nose*, 280.
tryded (trydedd), ord. num. f. *third, one of three*, 45–46 n., 95.
trydyd (trydydd), ord. num. m. *third, one of three*, 422, 436, 461.
tu m. *side, direction*, 398; **tu a**, *facing*, 437 n.
ty m. *house*, 56, 57, 152.
tylwyth m. *household, family*, 363.
tyrnassoed. See **teyrnas.**
tywyssawc m. *leader, noble, overlord*; pl. **tywyssogyon**, 242.

uab. See **mab.**
uaeth. See **maeth.**
uagyssant. See **magu.**
ual (fal). See **mal.**
uam. See **mam.**
uanagyssant. See **menegi.**
uann. See **ban(n).**
uchel adj. *high*, 29; compar. **uch**, 24, used as prep. *above*; used with **penn** in the phrases **uch penn, uch benn (uwchben)**, *above*, 4, 29, 157; eq. **kyuuch (kyf-uch)**, *as high*, 180.
ucheneit (ucheneid) f. *sigh*, 408.
uchot (uchod) adv. *above*, 66.
udunt. See **y** 2.

VOCABULARY

ue = **uy (fy)**, 306.
uedei. See **medu**.
uedwl. See **medwl**.
uedylyssant. See **medwl**.
uegin. See **megin**.
uei. See **bot**.
ueirych. See **march**.
ueis. See **beis**.
uelly (felly). See **yuelly**.
uerch. See **merch**.
ulwydyn. See **blwydyn**.
un 1. *one, any,* 23, 79, 80.
    2. (*the*) *same,* 5, 116, 218.
    3. *one former,* 135.
unben m. *leader, chief, man of rank,* 133.
uo. See **bo**.
uod. See **bot**.
uon. See **bon**.
uonllwm. See **bonllwm**.
uorbennyd. See **morben**.
uorwyn. See **morwyn**.
uot. See **bot**.
urawt. See **brawt**.
urdaul = **urddasol**, *honourable, noble,* 448 n.
ureint. See **breint**.
ureithell. See **breithell**.
urenhin(aeth). See **brenhin(aeth)**.
uroder. See **broder**.
urodyr. See **brawt**.
uu, uuant, uuassei, uuwyt, mut. of **bu**, &c. See **bot**.
uwrw. See **bwrw**.
uwy, uwyaf (len. of **mwyaf**). See **mawr**.
uwyt(a). See **bwyt(a)**.
uy. See **fy**.
uychanet. See **bychan**.
uyd mut. of **byd**. See **bot**.
uydaf, uydwch, uydynt. See **bot**.
uyg = **fy**+**g** = **ng**, indicating nas. mut. of foll. word, 173, 174.
uyghanyat. See **fy** and **canyat**.
uym (fym), fy+**m** indicating nas. mut. of foll. word, 273, 276.
uyn(n). See **mynnu**.
uynet. See **mynet**.
uynhei, uynhir, uynhynt, uynnhei. See **mynnu**.
uynyd in the phrase **y uynyd (i fynydd)** adv. phrase, *up,* 25, 364.
uys, uyssed. See **bys**.
uyw. See **byw**.

VOCABULARY

vu, 42v. See **bot**.
vwyt, 439v.
vy, 260 (= **wy**).

waeth. See **drwc**.
wahard. See **gwahard**.
want. See **gwant**.
waradwyd(aw). See **gwaradwyd(aw)**.
waret. See **gwaret**.
warth. See **gwarth**.
was. See **gwas**.
wastat. See **gwastat**.
wayret. See **gwaered**.
wdost(i). See **gwybot**.
wedy. See **gwedy**.
wei mut. of **bei**. See **bot**.
weilgi. See **gweilgi**.
weisson. See **gwas**.
weithon adv. *now*, 222.
welaf, weled, welsant, welsynt, wely, welynt. See **gwelet**.
well mut. of **gwell**. See **da**.
wenn. See **gwyn(n)**.
whaer, 70v. See **chwaer**.
wiscaw. See **gwiscaw**.
wlat. See **gwlat**.
wled. See **gwled**.
wn. See **gwybod**.
wnaeth, wnaethant, -ont, wnaethpwyt, wnaf, wnant, wnathoedit, wnelit, wnelych, wneuthur. See **gwneuthur**.
wr. See **gwr**.
wragedd. See **gwreic**.
wreic. See **gwreic**.
wres. See **gwres**.
wrth prep. *to, as far as*, 74, 75, 136; *because of*, 145; prep. prons. based on **wrth**: 2 sg. **wrthyt**, 34; 3 sg. m. **wrthaw**, 41; 2 pl. **wrthywch**, 30; 3 pl. **wrthunt**, 204; **y wrth**, *concerning*, 154, 269; *compared to*, 429; prep. pron. based on **y wrth**: 3 sg. f. **iwrthi (y wrthi)**, 429.
wy indep. pers. pron. 3 pl. *they*, 21, 31, 68; **wynt**, 13 n., 31, 34; **hwy**, 187, is a later form.
wybuant, wybuwyt. See **gwybot**.
wyd. See **gwyd**.
wydat. See **gwybot**.
wydwic. See **gwydwic**.
wydyat, 419v.
wynabwarth, 113v. See **wynepwerth**.
wyneb m. *face*, 114.

wynepwerth m. *honour-price*, 113 n.
wynnyas. See **gwyn(n)yas.**
wynt. See **wy.**
wynteu conjunctive pers. pron. 3 pl., 27, 28, 183; **wynte**, 445.
wyntwy indep. pers. pron. (doubled) 3 pl., 167.
wypo. See **gwybod.**
wyr. See **gwr.**
wys. See **gwys.**
wysc. See **gwysc.**
wyt. See **bot.**
wythuet (wythfed) ord. num. *eighth*, 403.

y 1. def. art. *the*, 4, 30, 32. See also **yr.**
y 2. (Mod. W. **i**) prep. *to, for*, 7, 17, 28; expressing purpose, 18, 36. 47; in phrase **e(= y) ymdeith**, *away*, 92; prep. prons. based on **y**: 1 sg. **ym**, 84, 95, 98, **im**, 149, 162, 169; (emphatic) **ymi**, 148, 162, 381; 2 sg. **yt, it, id,** *to thee*, 85, 101, 137, 140 (*of thine*); (emphatic) **yti**, 148, 156, **ytti**, 81 v., 101 v.; 3 sg. m. **idaw, ydaw**, 88, 143, 145; f. **idi (iddi)**, 165, 210, 220; 2 pl. **ywch**, 29, 261, 395; 3 pl. **udunt** (Mod. W. **iddynt**), 59, 74, 127.
y 3. (len.) dep. pers. pron. 3 sg. m. *his*, 5, 34, 109; written **e**, 42; 3 sg. f., 72, 83; 3 pl. 74, 439.
y 4. affirm. part., preceding the verb (used before consonants), 6, 37, 48. See also **mal y(d).**
y 5. (= **yn**), *in* (used predicatively as a particle), 242, 178 n., 411, 436.
y 6. For **y** in combination with other preps., see the other prep., e.g. **y dan**, see **dan.** (**y** < **de,** *from*).
'y inf. obj. pers. pron. 3 sg., 90.
y'r (i'r), *to the*, 28, 33, 39.
y'th, *in thy*, 149, 303.
ych (Mod. W. **eich**) dep. pers. pron. 2 pl. *your*, 308, 315.
ychwanegu vn. *add, increase, enlarge*; *addition*, &c., 136.
yd rel. part., used before verbs, *that*, 12; with **lle**, *where*, 28, 106.
yd (ydd) affirm. part., used before vowels, and preceding the verb, 2, 56, 91.
yg, y, *in*+**g** representing nas. mut. of foll. **k-**, 214, 232, 234.
yGlan (yng Nglan), y, *in* (nas.)+ **Glan**, 409.
ygwaelawt, y(n)g(**y,** *in*+ **(n)g** indicating nas. mut.)+ **gwaelawt**, q.v.
yll dep. prefixed pers. pron. 3 pl., 473 n.
ym. See **y** 2.
ym prep. *in* (form used before **p**), 64, 194.
ym (= **fym**), 173 n.
ym(m)a (yma) adv. *here*, 31, 31 v., 69.
ymadaw (a) vn. *depart (from), quit*; past 3 sg. **ymedewis**, 345.
ymadrawd (ymadrawdd), m. *conversation, speech*, 121.

VOCABULARY

ymanodi (ym-anod(d)i) vn. *penetrate, sink (mutually)*, 336–7 n.

ymaruar (ymarwar) vn. *discuss* (the simple verb is **arwar**, *delight, entertain*), 63.

ymchoelut, ymchwelut vn. *return*; past 3 sg. **ymchwelwys**, 105 n.; 3 pl. **ymchoelassant**, 105 v.

ymdanunt. See **am**.

ymdeith vn. *go away, journey*; in phrase **e ymdeith**, *away*, 92, 207 (cf. syntax of Sc. G. **air falbh**).

ymdidan (ymddiddan) m. *conversation, talking*, 26, 59, 130.

ymdidanwr m. *talker, conversationalist*, 135.

ymdiwallu vn. *supply* or *satisfy (oneself)*, 426.

ymedyryaw vn. *push in, creep in*, 382.

ymeith, 92 v., 207 v. See **ymdeith**.

ymgaru vn. *love one another*; imperf. 3 pl. **ymgerynt**, 12.

ymglywet vn. *hear one another, hear mutually*; imperf. subj. (in clause expressing purpose) 3 pl. **ymglywynt**, 26.

ymgyuathrachu (ymgyfathrachu) vn. *unite (by marriage), ally (oneself)*, 36 n.

ymgyuoc, 369 v. (n.).

ymgyuot (ymgyfod, Mod. W. **ymgyfodi)** vn. *rise*, 369 n.

ymherued (ym+perfedd m. *middle), in the middle*, 187.

ymi. See **y** 2.

ymlad (ymladd) m. *fighting, battle*, 11, 166, 177 n.

ymlaen adv. *at the front of, at the head of* 331; **ym blaen**, 331v.

ymlith prep. *among*, 382; **ym plith**, 382v.

ymodwrd (ymodwrdd) m. *tumult, murmuring of dissatisfaction* **(ym-go-twrdd,** cf. Ir. **dord,** *noise*), 213.

ymrwymaw vn. *bind (together)*, 37.

ymtiryoni (a) vn. *show friendship (to), deal kindly (with)*, 360.

ymuadeu (ymfaddeu < ym + maddeu) vn. *part oneself from* (foll. by **a(c)**), 173. Cf. Mod. W. **maddau**.

ymwaret (ymwared) m. *deliverance*, 107.

ymwelet (ymweled) vn. *visit* (foll. by **a(c)**, *with*), 118, 205.

ymysc prep. *amid, among*; in the phrase **ymysc hynny**, *in the meantime*, 207.

ymywn (Mod. W. **(i) mewn**) prep. and adv. *inside, within*, 56, 57, 317; **mywn**, 57v.

yn prep. *in*, used predicatively as a particle, with the vn. and other nouns, adjj., and adverbs (Ir. **i n-**; cf. also the use of O.Ir. **oc** or Sc. G. **ag**), 3, 71, 87; also used as adv. part. with adjj., 40, 59, 107; sometimes appearing as **y** in the W.B. version, e.g. **y barawt**, 178 n.

yn prep. *in, into*, 3, 42, 46; in the phrases **hyt yn,** *to, as far as;* **yn . . . ol,** *after . . .*, 109, 111; prep. prons. based on **yn**: 3 sg. m. **yndaw (ynddaw),** 142v., 322; f. **yndi (ynddi),** 278.

yn (Mod. W. **ein**) dep. pers. pron. 1 pl. *our*, 310.

yn yd, *while*, 372.

yna adv. *there, then*, 68, 129, 165.
yneuad, neuad (**yneuadd**, &c.) f. *hall*, 127, 435. See 30 n.
ynghylch prep. *round about*, 6.
ynheu conjunctive indep. pers. pron. 1 sg., 117v.
yniuer (**ynifer**) m. and f. *number, retinue*, 30 n., 42, 252; pl. **yniueroed** (**yniferoedd**), 48, 49, **niueroed**, 42 v., 48 v., 350.
yno adv. *there, thither*, 149, 179, 399.
ynteu conjunctive indep. pers. pron. 3 sg. m., 8, 39, 55.
yny conj. *until*, 50, 145, 186; **yny uyd** (**fydd**), *until (it) is*, 186, 187–8. See also 365 n.
ynys f. *island*, 1, 38, 46.
yr 1. def. art. (before vowels or **h-**), 1, 35, 40.
    2. variant form of perfective vb. part., 69, 80 n.; **'r**, 94.
    3. (Mod. W. **er**) prep. *because of, on account of*, 135.
    4. (Mod. W. **er**) prep. *notwithstanding*, 439 n., 440.
ys 1. the copula, *it is*, 362.
    2. verbal part. (without distinctive force), 307.
    3. inf. obj. pers. pron. 3 sg., 92 n.
yscraff (**ysgraff**) f. *a small boat, ferry-boat*; pl. **yscraffeu**, 223 n.
yscwyd (**ysgwydd**) f. *shoulder*, 189, 233, 374.
yspadawt (**ysbaddawd**) m. *guest-hall* (?), 479.
yspeit (Mod. W. **ysbaid**) m. *space of time*, 442.
yspydawt (**ysbyddawd**) f. *feast* (?); *company, assembly* (?), 448 n.; **yspydaut**, 482.
yssit, *there is*, 347–9 n.
yssyd. See **bot**.
ystauell (**ystafell**) f. *chamber*, 178, 179, 184.
ystlys f. *side*, 276 (Ir. **sliss**).
ystryw m. and f. *trick, stratagem*, 328.
ystynnu vn. *invest*, 303; past impers. **ystynnwyt**, 353.
yt, yt(t)i. See **y** 2.
ytoedynt. See **bot**.
yu (Mod. W. **i'w**), **y** 2.+**'u** inf. pron. 3 pl., 167.
yuelly (**yfelly**) adv. *so, thus*, 13, 70, 76; also **uelly**, 76 v., 221 v., 226v.
yuet (**yfed**) vn. *drink*, 427.
yw. See **bot**.
ywch. See **y** 2.

PERSONAL NAMES

Anarawc, 89, 246. In 246 called **Anarawc Walltgrwn.**
Beli, son of Mynogan, 8 n., 414.
Bendigeiduran (Bendigeidfran), son of Llyr, 1, 50, 57 *et passim.*
Bran, 242, 245, 479.
Branwen, daughter of Llyr, 1 n., 36, 45, &c.; **Bronwen,** 95 n.
Caswallawn (Caswallon), son of Beli, 414 n., 417, 419.
Cradawc (Cradawg), son of Bran, 242, 245, 250; **Caradawc,** 416 v.
Efnyssyen, uterine brother of Bendigeiduran, 6, 65, 331.
Eruyll (Erfyll), 247.
Eue(h)yd Hir, Hefeydd Hir, 90, 110, 245.
Eurosswyd, father of Nissyen and Efnyssyen, 8, 357.
Fodor uab Eruyll (Ffodor fab Erfyll), 246.
Gliuieri (Glifieri), 389 v.
Gliuieu Eil Taran, Glifieu son of Thunder, 389 n.
Grudyeu (Gruddieu), son of Muriel, 390.
Guern (Gwern), son of Matholwch, 302, 371.
Gwydel (Gwyddel), Irishman, 339, 342, 384; dual, 383; pl. **Gwydyl,** 328, 335, 375.
Gwyn Hen, 390, 450.
Heilyn, son of Gwyn Hen, 390, 450.
Idic (Iddig), son of Anarawc, 89, 246.
Kymidei Kymeinuoll, Big-bellied Battler (?), 151.
Llashar uab Llayssar Llaesgygwyt (Llaesgyngwyd), 247-8.
Llassar Llaes Gyfnewit, 150.
Llyr, father of Bendigeiduran, Branwen, and Manawydan, 1 n., 37, 53.
Mallolwch 298 v. (n.)
Manawydan, son of Llyr, 4, 53, 110.
Matholwch, king of Ireland, 32, 45, 49.
Mordwyd Tyllyon (Morddwyd T.), 371, 372.
Muryel (Muriel), 390.
Mynogan, father of Beli, 8.
Nissyen, uterine brother of Bendigeiduran, 5, 10, 357.
Penardun, mother of Bendigeiduran, Manawydan, &c.; daughter of Beli son of Mynogan, 8 n.
Pendaran Dyuet, Pendaran of Dyfed, 248; **Pendarar,** 423.
Pryderi, 389 n.
Rhiannon, 395.
Talyessin, 389.
Unic Glew Yscwyd, Unig of the Strong Shoulder, 110, 246.
Wlch Min-asgwrn, Wlch Bone-lip, 247 n.
Ynawc (Ynawg), 390.

PLACE-NAMES

Aber Alau (Alaw), 404.
Aber Henuelen (Henfelen), 398, 453; the W form is **Henueleu.**
Aberfraw (Aberffraw), 49, 51, 52.
Abermenei, the *aber* of the Menai, 202.
Archan, name of a river, 254.
Ardudwy, 3 n.
Cernyw, Cornwall, 399, 453.
Edeirnon, 243 n.
Freinc, France, 393.
Glan Alaw, 409.
Guales (Gwales), 397 n.; **Gualas,** 434.
Gwynuryn (Gwynfryn), The White Hill, 392, 460.
Hardlech (Harddlech), Harlech, 3, 394, 410.
Iwerdon (Iwerddon), Ireland, 14, 32, 38; **Ynys Iwerdon,** 350–1.
Kaer Seint yn Aruon, Caernarvon, 232 n.
Kymry, the Welsh; Wales, 214, 223, 231.
Lli, name of a river, 254.
Llinon, the river Shannon, 285–6 n.
Llundein, London, 2, 392, 401.
Llyn y Peir, The Lake of the Cauldron, 157.
Penuro (Penfro), 397, 434.
Seith Marchawc, 244 n.
Tal Ebolyon, 146 n., 404.
Ynys y Kedeirn, The Island of the Mighty, 38 n., 53; **Kedyrn,** 272.

PRINTED IN GREAT BRITAIN
AT THE UNIVERSITY PRESS, OXFORD
BY VIVIAN RIDLER
PRINTER TO THE UNIVERSITY